Mediumship and Spirit Communication

A Comprehensive Guide to Psychic Development, Shamanism, Spiritualism, Voodoo, and Connecting with Spirit Guides, Ancestors, Archangels, and Angels

© **Copyright 2024 - All rights reserved.**

The content contained within this book may not be reproduced, duplicated, or transmitted without direct written permission from the author or the publisher.

Under no circumstances will any blame or legal responsibility be held against the publisher, or author, for any damages, reparation, or monetary loss due to the information contained within this book, either directly or indirectly.

Legal Notice:

This book is copyright protected. It is only for personal use. You cannot amend, distribute, sell, use, quote, or paraphrase any part, or the content within this book, without the consent of the author or publisher.

Disclaimer Notice:

Please note the information contained within this document is for educational and entertainment purposes only. All effort has been executed to present accurate, up-to-date, reliable, and complete information. No warranties of any kind are declared or implied. Readers acknowledge that the author is not engaging in the rendering of legal, financial, medical, or professional advice. The content within this book has been derived from various sources. Please consult a licensed professional before attempting any techniques outlined in this book.

By reading this document, the reader agrees that under no circumstances is the author responsible for any losses, direct or indirect, that are incurred as a result of the use of the information contained within this document, including, but not limited to, errors, omissions, or inaccuracies.

Your Free Gift
(only available for a limited time)

Thanks for getting this book! If you want to learn more about various spirituality topics, then join Mari Silva's community and get a free guided meditation MP3 for awakening your third eye. This guided meditation mp3 is designed to open and strengthen ones third eye so you can experience a higher state of consciousness. Simply visit the link below the image to get started.

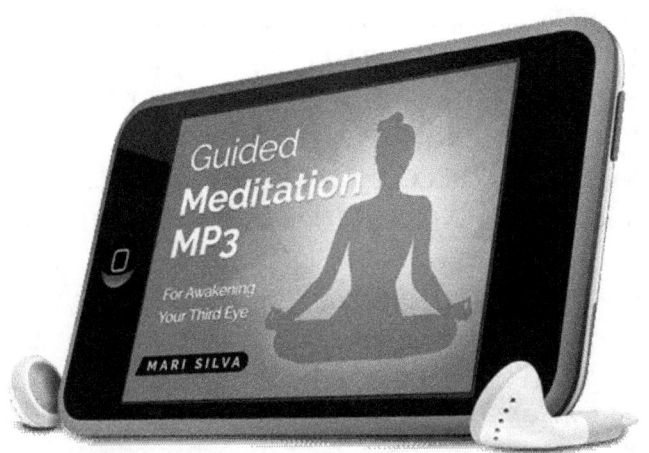

https://spiritualityspot.com/meditation

Table of Contents

PART 1: MEDIUMSHIP FOR BEGINNERS 1
   INTRODUCTION 2
   CHAPTER 1: THE WAY OF THE MEDIUM 4
   CHAPTER 2: YOUR ASTRAL BODY AND THE SPIRIT WORLD 13
   CHAPTER 3: GROUNDING AND PREPARATION 22
   CHAPTER 4: HOW TO RECOGNIZE ENERGY 31
   CHAPTER 5: DEVELOPING CLAIRVOYANCE AND OTHER CLAIRS 40
   CHAPTER 6: SPIRIT CHANNELING 101 50
   CHAPTER 7: CHANNEL YOUR SPIRIT GUIDES 59
   CHAPTER 8: CLEANSING AND PROTECTING YOURSELF 68
   CHAPTER 9: THE POWER OF SCRYING 77
   CHAPTER 10: ADVANCED SPIRIT WORLD COMMUNICATION METHODS 86
   CONCLUSION 93
PART 2: SPIRIT COMMUNICATION 95
   INTRODUCTION 96
   CHAPTER 1: CAN WE REALLY COMMUNICATE WITH THE SPIRITS? 98
   CHAPTER 2: TAPPING INTO YOUR PSYCHIC ABILITIES 108
   CHAPTER 3: GETTING READY FOR SPIRIT WORK 119
   CHAPTER 4: CHANNELING THE SPIRITS 126
   CHAPTER 5: SPIRITUAL TOOLS AND HOW TO USE THEM 135

CHAPTER 6: WORKING WITH ANCESTORS AND DEPARTED LOVED ONES 142
CHAPTER 7: CONNECT TO YOUR SPIRIT GUIDES 150
CHAPTER 8: CONTACTING ANGELS 157
CHAPTER 9: REACHING OUT TO ARCHANGELS 164
CHAPTER 10: CLEANSING AND DEFENSIVE METHODS 172
CONCLUSION 183
HERE'S ANOTHER BOOK BY MARI SILVA THAT YOU MIGHT LIKE 185
YOUR FREE GIFT (ONLY AVAILABLE FOR A LIMITED TIME) 186
REFERENCES 187

Part 1: Mediumship for Beginners

An Essential Guide to Psychic Development, Clairvoyance, Scrying, and Channeling in Shamanism, Spiritualism, and Voodoo

Introduction

Do you want to develop your mediumship skills? Are you curious about the spirit world and how you can communicate with spirits? If so, this guide will teach you everything you need to know about communicating with the spirit world.

Developing your mediumship skills can be a rewarding and life-changing experience. It can also be a bit daunting, especially if you're just starting. This guide will ease you into the world of mediumship and provide you with all the information and resources you need to get started. You first need to understand that everyone can communicate with spirits. We were all born with this ability, but it is dormant for many of us. The good news is that it can be awakened. There are many different ways to develop your mediumship skills. While some people can effortlessly communicate with spirits, others must work harder to develop this innate skill.

One of the best ways to develop your mediumship skills is to find a mentor. A mentor is someone who has already developed their mediumship skills and who can help guide you on your journey. A good mentor will be able to teach you how to ground and protect yourself, how to recognize energy, and how to develop your clairs. Another great way to develop your mediumship skills is to study. There are many books and resources available on the topic of mediumship. Reading about different techniques and methods will help you develop your skills further. Many online courses can teach you about mediumship.

In "Mediumship for Beginners," you'll learn about the different types of mediumship, how to develop your mediumship skills, and how to communicate with spirits. The first section of this guide will introduce you to the basics of mediumship, including what it is and how it works. We'll also discuss different ways to develop your mediumship skills. In the second section, we'll explore the spirit world and teach you how to communicate with spirits. You'll also discover how to protect yourself from negative energy and how to cleanse and protect your space. Finally, we'll cover advanced topics, such as scrying and channeling.

To help you get started on your journey, we have included chapters covering the basics of mediumship, including how to recognize energy, develop your clairs, and scry. We have also included a chapter on advanced spirit communication methods. We hope you enjoy this guide and that it helps you to develop your mediumship skills. Whether you're just beginning your journey as a medium or looking to brush up on your skills, this informative guide will provide you with everything you need to know about communicating with the spirit world. So, let's get started!

Chapter 1: The Way of the Medium

Have you ever wondered whether or not communicating with the dead was possible? If so, you're not alone. Throughout history, man has attempted to contact the spirit world in various ways. This practice is known as mediumship. This can be defined as the ability to communicate with the dead or spirits. Mediums have this ability, and they use it to relay messages from the spirit world to the living.

Mediumship is the ability to communicate with spirits.
https://www.pexels.com/photo/assorted-tarot-cards-on-table-3088369/

Mediumship has been around since the dawn of time and has taken many different forms. In the early days, mediumship was often associated with shamanism and witchcraft. As time went on, however, it began to take on a more spiritualistic approach. This chapter will explore the history of mediumship and the different types that exist today. It will also introduce you to some genuine mediums working in the modern world.

What Is Mediumship?

Mediumship is the ability to communicate with spirits. This can be done in several ways, including through auditory or visual means. All people are born with the natural ability to connect with the dead, while some may need to develop their skills through practice and study. Mediums often use their abilities to provide comfort and closure to those who have lost loved ones. They may also be able to offer insights into the future or guidance on important life decisions. While some people are skeptical of mediumship, many believe it is a real and valuable gift.

By definition, a medium acts as an intermediary between the living and the dead. Mediums can bridge the gap between our world and the spirit world. They use their abilities to communicate with spirits and relay messages to the living. Mediums may also be able to see into the future or offer guidance on important life decisions. With their help, we can connect with our loved ones who have passed on and receive closure or comfort.

Abilities of a Medium

Communicating with the dead has been practiced since ancient times. To become a medium, you must first learn about the different abilities required for the job. One of the most essential abilities is that of clairvoyance or clear seeing. This allows the medium to see beyond the physical world and into the spirit realm. Another ability is clairaudience or clear hearing. This allows the medium to hear messages from the other side that are not normally audible to the human ear. In addition, mediums often have a strong sense of empathy, which allows them to feel the emotions of those who have passed on. By honing these skills, anyone can become a medium and help to connect with those who have died.

Mediumship Now and Then

In the past, mediums often worked as part of a spiritualist church, holding séances and conducting readings for the public. However, the use of mediumship began to decline in the early 20th century as people became more skeptical of the practice. In recent years, however, mediumship is more often seen as a personal practice. Many people use mediumship to connect with loved ones who have passed away, and some even use it to communicate with animals or other beings. As our world becomes more open to different spiritual belief systems, mediumship will likely continue to grow in popularity. Who knows what kind of amazing connections we'll make in the future?

Early History

Mediumship is a topic that has fascinated people for centuries. The early history of mediumship is shrouded in mystery, but there are some interesting theories about its origins. One theory suggests that mediumship developed as a way to contact the spirit world and gain guidance and wisdom from beyond. Others believe it is a natural human ability that various cultures have harnessed throughout history. Regardless of its origins, mediumship has played an essential role in many cultures and continues to do so today. Thanks to modern communication technology, anyone can now experience its wonders by connecting with a trusted psychic medium.

Spiritualism

During the 19th century, spiritualism became popular throughout the United States and Europe. At its core, spiritualism believes in the ability to communicate with the dead, and many people turned to mediums to receive messages from loved ones who had passed away. In addition to providing comfort and closure for grieving individuals, spiritualism also played a significant role in the development of mediumship.

Through their work with spirits, mediums began to develop heightened psychic abilities, which they then used to help others connect with the other side. As mediumship became more widely accepted, it became a legitimate form of communication, paving the way for future psychic research. Today, spiritualism is still practiced by millions of people worldwide, and its impact on religion and psychic research can still be felt.

Shamanism

Shamanism is a type of spiritual practice based on the belief that everything in the universe is connected. Shamans are spiritual guides who heal individuals and communities by connecting with the spirit world. To do this, they must first enter into a trance-like state, which allows them to travel to different planes of existence. Once they have made contact with the spirits, they can relay messages and advice that can help heal those in need.

Shamanism is an ancient practice that has been used by indigenous cultures all over the world. It is only in recent years, however, that shamanism has begun to enter the mainstream. As more people become interested in alternative forms of healing, shamanism is likely to continue to grow in popularity. If you're looking for a deeper connection to the spiritual world, shamanism may be the path for you.

Voodoo

Voodoo is a religion that originated in Haiti, but it has since spread to other parts of the world, including the United States. It is based on the belief that there is a spirit world that can interact with our own. Voodoo practitioners work with these spirits, or *loas*, to bring about positive change in their lives. They may also turn to the spirits for guidance and protection.

Voodoo is often associated with dark and black magic, but this is unrealistic. It is a religion that should be respected, just like any other. If you are interested in learning more, there are many resources available. Just remember to approach it with an open mind and a respectful attitude. Voodoo has always been a controversial topic. Some say it is the dark side of mediumship, while others claim it is simply another way to connect with the spirit world.

Modern Times

Nowadays, anyone can experience the wonder of mediumship by connecting with a trusted psychic medium. There are many different ways to do this, including online chat rooms, phone readings, and in-person sessions. No matter how you choose to connect, you can be sure that you'll receive accurate and helpful information from your medium.

If you are interested in connecting with a loved one who has passed away or simply want to get in touch with your spirituality, mediumship is a great way to do it. With the help of a psychic medium, you can explore the depths of your soul and discover answers to the questions that have been weighing heavily on your mind.

The Different Types of Mediumship

There are different types of mediumship, each with its unique skill set. Some mediums can see and speak to ghosts, while others can only communicate with them through psychometry, which is the ability to read objects touched by the deceased. Other mediums can channel the dead, allowing the ghosts to possess their bodies to speak through them. Finally, some mediums can astral project, leaving their bodies and traveling to the spirit world. Each type of mediumship has its strengths and weaknesses, and it is up to each medium to decide which type of communication is best for them.

1. Physical Mediumship

Physical mediumship is one of the most fascinating and controversial forms of mediumship. Physical mediums can materialize "spiritual beings" and produce other physical phenomena, such as levitation and teleportation. This type of activity is often associated with séances and Spiritualism, and it has been the subject of intense scientific scrutiny. Some physical mediums have been exposed as frauds, while others have been scientifically validated. Whether you believe in the paranormal or not, physical mediumship remains one of the most intriguing phenomena in the world.

2. Mental Mediumship

Mental mediumship is a psychic ability in which the medium telepathically receives information from the spirit world. In other words, the medium does not use any physical senses to receive communication from the spirits. Instead, the information is passed on through thoughts and feelings. Mental mediumship is a relatively rare ability, but it can be beneficial for spirit communication.

One of the benefits of mental mediumship is that it allows the spirit to communicate directly with the medium without having to use an intermediary. This can provide a more direct and personal form of communication than other methods, such as using a Ouija board or talking to a psychic. Additionally, mental mediumship is not limited by distance like some other forms of communication. The medium can receive information from anywhere worldwide, regardless of how far away they are. Mental mediumship is a powerful tool for anyone interested in communicating with the spirit world.

3. Spiritualist Mediumship

Spiritualist mediums are exceptionally skilled at connecting with the spirits of those who have passed away. This ability allows them to provide comfort and closure to the bereaved by delivering messages from loved ones who have crossed over. Mediumship can also be used to communicate with ancestors or other guides who can offer wisdom and guidance. While some people may be skeptical, a growing body of evidence suggests it is a real and powerful phenomenon.

4. Trance Mediumship

Trance mediumship is a type of mediumship in which the medium enters into a trance state to commune with the spirit world. The trance state is characterized by an altered state of consciousness, during which the medium becomes unaware of his surroundings and is instead completely focused on spirit communication.

While in a trance, the medium may exhibit strange behaviors, such as speaking in tongues or experiencing convulsions. However, these behaviors are not considered to be under the medium's control. Instead, they are seen as a manifestation of the spirit's presence. Trance mediumship is considered one of the most potent and authentic forms, as it allows for a direct connection to the spirit world.

5. Channeling

Channeling is one of the most well-known methods of mediumship, and it involves receiving messages from spirit guides or other nonphysical beings. The channeler goes into a trance-like state, and the entity speaks through them, using its vocal cords to communicate. Many people who channel say they feel like they are channeling energy rather than actual words, and the experience can be both powerful and transformative. Channeling can be used for guidance, healing, or simply to receive messages from loved ones who have passed on. While becoming a channeler is not always easy, anyone can learn how to do it with practice and patience.

6. Automatic Writing

Automatic writing is a type of channeling in which the medium goes into a trance-like state and allows spirits to dictate messages through their hand. This can be done with a pen and paper or even using a keyboard. Many people who practice automatic writing claim that they can receive clear and concise messages from the other side, which can comfort those grieving. Automatic writing can also be used for divination purposes, as the messages received can offer insight into future events.

While anyone can try their hand at automatic writing, it is said that those who are naturally gifted at channeling are more likely to have success. Suppose you're interested in giving it a try. In that case, the best way to start is by sitting down in a quiet place with a pen and paper (or your laptop) and simply letting your hand move across the page or fingers across the keyboard. It may take some practice to get into the flow, but eventually, you should be able to receive messages from your deceased loved ones.

7. Direct Voice

One type of mediumship is called the direct voice. A direct voice medium channels a deceased loved one's voice – either in person or over the phone. The most famous example of a direct voice medium is Doris Stokes, who spoke to the dead through her television show in the 1970s and 1980s. People would call in, and she would relay messages from their deceased relatives.

Sometimes, the voices would speak through her directly, and at other times they would speak through a disembodied spirit she would see in the room. Direct voice mediumship is considered one of the most accurate forms of mediumship because it eliminates any possibility of fraud. If a medium is genuinely channeling a deceased loved one's voice, there is no way for them to fake it.

8. ITC

One lesser-known type of mediumship is known as ITC or instrumental trans communication. This refers to the communication between our world and other realms through technology. ITC mediums use tools like radios, computers, and even televisions to receive messages from the beyond. While many people are skeptical of this type of mediumship, some well-documented cases suggest it is real. For example, in the 1970s, a team of researchers in Switzerland recorded voices from the dead using a tape recorder. In more recent years, ITC mediums have used mobile phones and social media to communicate with the other side. Whether you believe in ITC or not, it is an exciting phenomenon worth exploring.

9. Electronic Voice Phenomenon

Electronic voice phenomenon, or EVP, is a mediumship type involving communication from the beyond through electronic devices. This can include radios, TVs, answering machines, and even cell phones. The voices heard during EVP are typically faint and difficult to understand, but they can occasionally be clear and distinct. Many people believe that EVP is a way for the dead to reach out to the living. There are countless stories of people receiving messages from loved ones who have passed away. While no scientific evidence supports this claim, EVP remains a popular phenomenon, with thousands of people worldwide reporting experiences with it.

10. Evidential Mediumship

Evidential mediumship is one type of mediumship that is focused on providing evidence of life after death. During an evidential mediumship reading, the medium will try to provide specific information about the spirit communicating, such as their name, relationship to the sitter, and what they want to say. The goal of evidential mediumship is to provide comfort and closure to the sitter by proving that life after death exists. If you are looking for a medium specializing in this type of reading, ask about their credentials and experience.

Real Mediums in Our Modern World

Many people today are interested in finding a genuine medium, especially in the modern world, where there is so much skepticism about anything that falls outside the realm of science. Some use Tarot cards or crystal balls, while others may simply go into a trance and allow the spirits to speak through them. Some claim to be able to channel messages from the dead, meaning they can receive messages from beyond the grave.

While it can be challenging to know whether or not a medium is truly gifted, there are certain signs you should look for. A good medium will usually have some kind of information about the person they are communicating with that they could not have otherwise known. They should also be able to provide specific details about the deceased, which others can verify. If you think you may have found a real medium, it is always best to get a second opinion from someone who is experienced in this field.

Scientific Proof

In recent years, there has been an increase in the number of people who claim to be able to contact the dead, and there is scientific evidence that this is indeed possible. One study by the University of Arizona showed that people who spoke to a medium could accurately describe details about their deceased loved ones, even when they had no prior knowledge of those details. This study provides strong evidence for the existence of mediums and their ability to communicate with the other side.

Today, there is a lot of skepticism surrounding the idea of mediums. However, there is also scientific proof that they exist and can communicate with the dead. This proof should be enough to convince even the most skeptical person that mediums are genuine and that they can provide us with valuable information about our loved ones who have passed away.

Mediumship is a centuries-old practice that has been used by people all over the world to communicate with their lost loved ones. There are many different types of mediumship, and each one has its unique way of providing evidence of life after death. While there is still much skepticism surrounding this topic, the increasing amount of scientific proof that mediums are real should be enough to convince even the most skeptical person.

With the help of a real medium, we can obtain closure and comfort by receiving messages from our loved ones who have passed away. This is an invaluable experience that can help us heal after the loss of a loved one. If you are interested in finding a real medium, ask about their credentials and experience. With the help of a gifted medium, you can obtain the closure and peace of mind you need.

Chapter 2: Your Astral Body and the Spirit World

If you are like most people, you have probably wondered what happens to us after we die. What becomes of our spirit? Is there an afterlife? And if so, what is it like? These are some of the questions that mediums seek to answer. Mediumship is the practice of communicating with the spirits of those who have passed on. To do this, mediums must first understand what the spirit is – and what the afterlife is like.

The subtle body is an energy field that surrounds and permeates the physical body.
https://www.pexels.com/photo/white-moon-on-hands-3278643/

According to many belief systems, the spirit is an immortal part of each of us that lives on after the physical body dies. The afterlife is often seen as a place where we can be reunited with our loved ones and enjoy eternal happiness. While there is much we do not yet know about the afterlife, mediums can provide us with valuable insights into this mystery through their unique ability to communicate with the spirits of those who have gone before.

This chapter will explore the nature of the spirit and the afterlife according to mediumship. We will begin by looking at the subtle body, which is often seen as the seat of the soul. We will then explore the astral body, which is believed to be the vehicle that carries our spirit after death. Next, we will examine how different belief systems perceive the soul. Finally, we will take a closer look at the afterlife and how mediums can help us to understand this mystery.

The Subtle Body

Most people are familiar with the physical body, but fewer are aware of the subtle body. The subtle body is an energy field that surrounds and permeates the physical body. It consists of the nadis, or energy channels, through which prana, or life force, flows. The subtle body also contains the chakras, or energy centers, through which prana is circulated.

The subtle body is often seen as the seat of the soul. It is a non-physical body that is believed to interpenetrate and extend beyond the physical body. The subtle body is composed of etheric, emotional, mental, and astral bodies. These bodies are believed to be constantly interacting with each other and the physical body.

The etheric body is the densest of the subtle bodies and is closest to the physical body; it is responsible for our physical health and vitality. The emotional body is composed of our feelings and emotions; it is in constant flux, changing as our emotions change. The mental body is composed of our thoughts and beliefs; it is the bridge between the physical and astral bodies.

Mediumship is the ability to perceive and work with the subtle body. Sensitive people can see the aura, or energy field, around another person. They can also feel the flow of prana in the nadis and chakras. By aligning their energies with those of another person, they can create a bridge between the physical and subtle bodies. This allows them to perceive and transmit messages from one level of consciousness to another. Mediums can also use their abilities to heal imbalances in the subtle body. By clearing blockages and restoring the flow of prana, they can promote physical, emotional, and spiritual wellness.

The Astral Body

According to the belief of mediumship, the soul leaves the physical body and enters into an astral body when people die. This astral body is made up of subtle energy which vibrates at a higher frequency than the physical world. With this astral body, we can travel to different realms and dimensions. There are also different vibration levels within the astral world, which may account for people's different experiences while in this state. For example, some people may only see colors, while others may see detailed landscapes.

The astral body is the lightest and most ethereal of the subtle bodies. It is believed to be our spirit body and the vehicle that carries our spirit after death. In some belief systems, the astral body is also known as the soul body. When we die, the astral body leaves the physical body behind and enters the afterlife. The astral body is often seen as a reflection of our true self. It is the part of us that is eternal and unchanging regardless of the vibration level; the astral world is said to be a place of peace and love. It is also believed that we can communicate with our loved ones who have passed on to the astral world. So next time you're wondering what happens after we die, remember that we may just be entering into another realm where we can explore and discover more about ourselves and the universe around us.

The Connection between the Astral Body and Spirit

Our astral body is our ethereal body; it is the vehicle of our soul and houses our consciousness. The astral body is connected to the physical body by a silver cord. This cord allows us to return to our physical bodies after we die. The astral body can also travel outside the physical body during sleep or in an out-of-body experience. Some people believe that the astral body is our true self and that the physical body is just a shell.

Our astral body contains our memories, thoughts, and feelings. It is made up of our spiritual energy. The astral dimension is a higher vibration than the physical dimension. Our astral body vibrates at a higher frequency than our physical body. This is why we can travel to different planes of existence and interact with other beings on these planes. Our spirit is the part of us that is eternal. It is who we are. Our spirit inhabits our astral body. It is what remains after we die and our physical bodies degrade back into the earth. Our spirit lives on in the spiritual realm.

How Different Practices See the Soul

Though the soul is a difficult concept to define, it is a central tenet of many religious and spiritual traditions. For some, the soul is an immortal essence that transcends the physical body, while others believe it is intimately bound up with our material existence. This varies from one tradition to the next, and there are many different ways of understanding the soul.

In Christianity, the soul is often seen as immortal and separate from the body. This means that when someone dies, their soul goes to either heaven or hell, depending on whether they have been good or bad during their life. In contrast, some Eastern philosophies see the soul as being intimately connected with the body.

Buddhism: The Soul Is Interconnected with All Things

Buddhism believes that we are reborn after death into different bodies, and our consciousness grows and develops over time. The soul is not seen as separate from the body in this tradition but rather as constantly changing and evolving. As you can see, many different understandings of the soul exist, and these differing beliefs can lead to very different practices.

Hinduism: The Soul Is Immanent

In Hinduism, the soul is seen as immanent, which means it is intimately bound up with the physical body. This does not mean that the soul is the same as the body but is a part of the body. The soul is seen as an essential part of our being; without it, we would not be able to function.

The soul is believed to be reborn into different bodies after death. This cycle of birth and death is known as samsara. Hinduism believes that the soul is trapped in samsara because of its desires and attachments. The only way to break free from this cycle is to achieve liberation or moksha. Moksha is a state of complete freedom from the cycle of birth and death.

Spiritualism

For spiritualists, the soul is the immaterial part of a human being that survives after death. This belief is based on the idea that there is more to life than just a physical body and the belief that we are all connected to a higher power. While scientific evidence cannot confirm the existence of the soul, many people find comfort in the idea that their loved ones are still with them in some way after they have passed away.

For spiritualists, the soul is not tied to any particular religion or belief system. Instead, it is a universal force connecting all living beings. This means that everyone has the potential to connect with the soul, regardless of their beliefs. The soul is seen as a source of wisdom and guidance, providing us with a path to follow in life. Ultimately, spiritualists believe that the soul is what makes us truly human and that it is our connection to the divine.

Shamanism

Shamanism is an ancient spiritual practice that has been practiced for centuries by indigenous cultures worldwide. At its core, shamanism is a way to connect with nature and the spirit world to promote healing and balance. Shamans believe everything in the universe is connected and that imbalances in the natural world can lead to illness and disharmony. One of the ways that shamans seek to restore balance is by working with the soul.

According to shamanic belief, the soul consists of three parts; the upper soul, lower soul, and middle soul. The upper soul is responsible for our spiritual connection to the divine, while the lower soul is responsible for our physical needs and desires. The middle soul acts as a bridge between the two, helping us to find harmony and balance in our lives. Shamans believe that when one of these parts of the soul becomes disconnected or imbalanced, it can lead to physical or psychological problems. By working with the soul, shamans can help to restore balance and harmony, promoting wellness on all levels.

Voodoo

In many cultures, the soul is seen as an ethereal entity that exists beyond the physical body. For voodoo practitioners, however, the soul is a very real and tangible force. To them, the soul is not just a spiritual essence but a physical one as well. This belief is based on the idea that the soul is composed of two parts; the *ti bon ange* and the *gros bon ange*.

The ti bon ange is the "little good angel" that resides within every person. It is responsible for our thoughts and emotions, and it is what gives us our individuality. The gros bon ange, on the other hand, is the "big good angel" that resides in the spirit world. It is responsible for our destiny, and it is what allows us to connect with the divine. Together, these two parts of the soul make up our entire being.

Afterlife

The concept of an afterlife has been a topic of discussion and debate for centuries. Some people believe there is life after death, while others contend that death is the end. There is no clear evidence either way, and it largely comes down to personal belief. Many religions have their own beliefs about what happens after death. Christians believe in heaven and hell, while Buddhists believe in reincarnation. There is no right or wrong answer, which ultimately comes down to each individual's beliefs. After all, we all have to die eventually, so it makes sense to think about what happens afterward. Regardless of what anyone believes, the concept of an afterlife will continue to be a source of fascination for centuries to come.

What Is the Afterlife?

The idea of an afterlife has been a source of comfort and hope for people throughout history. In many cultures, the belief in some form of life after death is central to religious teachings. For those who adhere to these beliefs, the afterlife is often seen as a place of reward or punishment, depending on their actions during this life. While the specifics may differ, the general idea is that the soul survives the body's death and goes on to another realm.

What that realm looks like is a matter of speculation, but it is often described as a paradise-like environment or a hellish one. Some believe there is reincarnation, while others hold that there is simply an end to consciousness. Whatever the case may be, the belief in an afterlife provides comfort for many in the face of death.

What Happens to Spirits When We Die?

There are many different beliefs about what happens to spirits when we die, but the one thing that everyone can agree on is that death is a mystery. Some believe that spirits go to a peaceful place where they can rest and watch over their loved ones. Others believe that spirits are reincarnated and come back as different people or animals. And still, others believe that spirits simply cease to exist after death. While we may never know for sure what happens to spirits when we die, it's comforting to know that there are many different beliefs about the afterlife. Whatever your beliefs may be, remember that death is a natural part of life, and there is no need to be afraid of it. Instead, embrace it as a part of the cycle of life and death.

Afterlife in Spiritualism

Spiritualists believe that the soul lives on after the physical body dies and that communication with the dead is possible. Proponents of this belief system often hold séances or use other forms of divination to connect with deceased loved ones. While some may view spiritualism as a way to scam unsuspecting people, many believe it is a legitimate way to connect with the other side. After all, if we have souls that live on after death, it stands to reason that they want to communicate with us. Whether or not you believe in spiritualism, it is an interesting way to think about the afterlife.

Afterlife in Shamanism

In shamanism, the afterlife is often seen as a journey through different realms. The soul is believed to travel to the underworld, facing challenges and transforming. After completing these trials, the soul is reborn into the spiritual world and given a new life. This cycle of death and rebirth is thought to continue until the soul reaches a state of enlightenment. Some shamans also believe it is possible to communicate with the dead, and they often use trance states to contact spirits in the spirit world. By understanding the afterlife, shamans can help their clients to make peace with death and prepare for their spiritual journey.

Afterlife in Voodoo Culture

In Voodoo culture, there is a strong belief in the afterlife. This belief is rooted in the idea that the soul is immortal and that it will continue to exist even after the body has died. The soul is seen as being locked inside the body, and it is only when the body dies that the soul can be released. Once released, the soul goes on to live in another realm known as the spirit world. In this world, the soul will be reunited with its ancestors and will be able to enjoy eternal happiness. The concept of reincarnation also plays a role in Voodoo's beliefs about the afterlife. It is believed that the soul can be reborn into another body and that this process will continue until the soul has attained perfection. Because of this, death is not seen as an ending but rather as a new beginning.

Peeking into the Afterlife

Most people have at least some curiosity about what happens after we die. It's only natural to wonder about the great unknown. Unfortunately, there's no way to know for sure what happens to us after we die. But that doesn't stop people from speculating. For many people, the thought of peeking into the afterlife is both intriguing and terrifying. It's an essential part of the human experience and helps us appreciate life all the more.

Many people believe that the afterlife is a mystery. Still, some say that it is possible to peek into the afterlife to find answers. Mediums are often able to communicate with the dead, and they may be able to provide information about what happens after death. While it is impossible to know for sure what happens after we die, talking to a medium may give you some peace of mind about what lies ahead. If you are curious about the afterlife, consider talking to a medium. They may just have the answers you are looking for.

The idea of mediumship – communicating with the dead – has been around for centuries. In recent years, however, it has become far more mainstream, thanks in part to shows like "Medium" and "The Long Island Medium." While some people are still skeptical about the validity of mediumship, many have had firsthand experience with the afterlife through the messages delivered by mediums.

For those who have lost loved ones, mediumship can provide much-needed closure. It can be difficult to come to terms with the fact that someone is no longer physically present in our lives. However, a message from beyond the grave can help to ease the pain of loss and provide comfort that our loved ones are still with us, even if we cannot see them.

In addition to providing comfort, mediumship can offer insights into the afterlife. What happens to us after we die? It is a question that has long intrigued people of all faiths. While there are many different beliefs about what happens to us after death, mediums who have communicated with the dead often report similar experiences. This suggests that there may be some truth to what they are saying.

Whether you believe in mediumship or not, it is impossible to deny that it has profoundly impacted many people's lives. For those who have suffered a loss, it can provide much-needed closure. For those curious about the afterlife, it can offer a glimpse into what may lie beyond this life. Whether you are a skeptic or a believer, mediumship is something worth exploring.

The astral body is a part of the human soul that is believed to be capable of traveling outside the physical body. It is connected to the spirit world and is said to be the source of our dreams and intuition. Mediums are people who can communicate with the dead and may be able to provide information about the afterlife. The idea of mediumship has been around for centuries, but it has become far more mainstream in recent years.

For those who have lost loved ones, mediumship can provide much-needed closure. It can also offer insights into the afterlife for those curious about what happens to us after we die. Whether you believe in mediumship or not, it is something worth exploring. Talking to a medium may give you peace of mind about what lies ahead. If you are curious about the afterlife, consider talking to a medium. They may just have the answers you are looking for.

Chapter 3: Grounding and Preparation

If you've ever been interested in mediumship, you know that it's not as simple as just talking to ghosts. A lot of preparation and work goes into it, both on the part of the medium and the person seeking to communicate with a loved one who has passed away. Without proper grounding and preparation, it's too easy to get caught up in the spiritual world without being able to control the situation or protect yourself from negative entities.

When it comes to mediumship, grounding and preparation are extremely essential.
https://www.pexels.com/photo/woman-in-white-shirt-holding-orange-and-white-lollipop-6943953/

In this chapter, we'll talk about the importance of grounding and preparation for mediumship. We will also discuss some simple but effective grounding exercises you can do to get started. We'll focus on the medium's side of things. Still, many of these tips can be applied to anyone looking to improve their connection with the "beyond." We'll also discuss ways to prepare your mind so that you're more receptive to messages from the other side.

The Importance of Grounding and Preparation

Mediumship is a skill that has been practiced for centuries, and it only recently began to gain mainstream acceptance. Despite its growing popularity, mediumship is still shrouded in mystery. Many people are unsure how to prepare for readings or what to expect. One of the most crucial things to remember is that mediumship is two-way communication.

The medium acts as a conduit between the physical and spiritual worlds. Still, it is up to the spirit to decide whether or not they want to communicate. This is why it is so essential to be properly prepared before readings. Grounding yourself will help you to feel more anchored and connected, making it easier for spirits to reach you. And taking some time to relax and clear your mind will make it easier for you to receive messages from the other side.

When it comes to mediumship, grounding and preparation are extremely essential. Here are some reasons why:

1. Helps You Stay Focused

As a medium, it is vital to be well-grounded and prepared before you begin readings. Grounding yourself will help you feel more connected to the physical world and prevent you from becoming overwhelmed by spirit energy. There are many different ways to ground yourself. Still, some common methods include visualizing roots growing from your feet into the earth or holding a piece of quartz in your hand. Once you feel firmly grounded, you can begin preparing for your reading. This may involve setting an intention, visualizing a protective bubble around yourself, or calling in your spirit guides. Taking the time to ground and prepare yourself before beginning a reading will help you stay focused and attuned to the messages you receive.

2. Increases Your Chances of Making Contact

Grounding yourself will help you feel more centered, making it easier to focus your mind and connect with the energies of the spirit world.

Preparation is also important, as it helps to clear your mind of any negative thoughts or emotions that could block your connection. When you are properly prepared, you are more likely to contact the spirit you seek to communicate with. It becomes easier for them to reach you and easier for you to receive their messages. By taking the time to ground and prepare yourself before a session, you'll increase your chances of making contact with the spirit world and receiving accurate messages.

3. Improves Your Connection

When it comes to mediumship, grounding and preparation are key to establishing a strong connection with the spirit world. Taking the time to ground yourself before you begin readings will help you clear your mind and focus your energy. This will allow you to be more receptive to the messages the spirit is trying to communicate. Similarly, preparing for readings by setting an intention and creating a sacred space can also help you connect more deeply with your guides and loved ones who have passed on. By taking the time to create a strong foundation, you'll be sure to get the most out of your mediumship reading.

4. Keeps You Safe from Negative Entities

As a medium, being well-grounded and prepared before you start to work will protect you from any negative entities that may try to attach themselves to you. There are a few simple things that you can do to make sure that you are safe before you begin readings. First, set the intention that only positive and highest good can come through. This will keep out any lower energies trying to attach themselves to you. Secondly, call in your spirit guides and ask them to surround and protect you. You can also imagine a white light surrounding you, creating a protective barrier against any negative energy.

Always say a prayer or meditate before you start working. This will help to raise your vibration levels and keep you in a positive state of mind. Wearing protective clothing such as a white robe or pendant will create a barrier between you and any negative energy. Finally, always work in a clean and clutter-free space. This will help create a calm and safe environment for you to work in. These simple tips can keep you safe from negative entities when working as a medium.

5. Helps You Manage Your Energy

Grounding yourself before you begin readings will help you to manage your energy and prevent you from becoming overwhelmed by the spirit world. When properly grounded, you can work more effectively as a medium and avoid burnout. Remember that you don't have to be always available to the spirit world. You can take breaks when you need to and return to your readings when you feel more centered.

Grounding Exercises

Mediumship grounding is a technique used to help mediums connect with the spirit world while remaining grounded in the physical world. The goal is to create a bridge between the two worlds so that communication can flow freely. There are many different ways to ground oneself. Still, some of the most common methods include visualization, meditation, and energy work.

When done properly, grounding can help to prevent psychic overload and promote clear and accurate communication with spirits. Not all mediums are the same, so finding a grounding method that works best for you is crucial. With practice, you'll be able to achieve a deeper connection with the spirit world while remaining fully present in the physical world.

1. The Tree Method

Many people new to mediumship are unaware of the different ways of grounding. One easy way to ground yourself is to imagine roots growing from the soles of your feet, anchoring you to the earth. Another method is to imagine yourself as a tree, with your feet rooted firmly in the ground and your arms reaching up toward the sky. This exercise can be done anywhere and only takes a few minutes. It is a great way to center yourself before beginning readings and can also be used to release excess energy after a session. Give it a try the next time you are feeling scattered or ungrounded.

2. The Balloon Method

There are several different exercises you can do to help you practice grounding. One such exercise is known as the balloon method. To try it out, sit comfortably and take a few deep breaths. Then, imagine that you are holding a balloon in your hand. Once you have a clear image of the balloon, mentally inflate it until it is about the size of a grapefruit. As you do so, mentally repeat the words, "I am expanding my mediumship abilities." Once the balloon is inflated, visualize it floating up into the air and then popping. As it does, feel your mediumship abilities expanding. This exercise can be done as often as you like, and with practice, you'll find that it becomes easier and more effective. Who knows - with enough practice, you may just be able to pop that balloon without even using your hands!

3. The Stone Method

Another simple way to ground yourself is with a stone. Start by finding a stone that feels comfortable to hold. It can be any size or shape, and it should be smooth so that it's easy to hold. Once you have your stone, sit down in a comfortable position and close your eyes. Take a few deep breaths and focus on the feel of the stone in your hand. Imagine roots growing from the stone and anchoring you to the earth. Visualize the roots going deep into the ground, spreading outward, and holding you securely in place.

As you focus on the roots, you should feel yourself becoming more grounded and present in the physical world. If you start feeling lightheaded or dizzy, open your eyes and take a few deep breaths until you feel better. Once you're grounded, you can put the stone down and continue your day. Grounding exercises like this one can help to protect you from negative energies and prevent you from becoming overwhelmed during a reading.

4. The Earthing Method

If you've ever felt disconnected, spaced out, or "not all there," it could be that you're not properly grounded. To remedy this, try the earthing method. Sit or stand with your feet planted firmly on the ground, and imagine roots growing from the soles of your feet deep into the earth below. Visualize these roots anchoring you to the planet, and focus on the sensation of being solidly connected. You should feel more present and focused after just a few minutes. If you don't have time to do a full grounding exercise, simply take a few deep breaths and visualize your feet rooted to the ground. This will help to center and ground you so that you can fully engage with the world around you.

5. The Visualization Method

One of the most effective methods to ground yourself is the visualization method. To do this exercise, find a comfortable place to sit or lie down. Close your eyes and take a few deep breaths. Visualize that a bright white light surrounds you. This light is cleansing and purifying, and it surrounds you with protection.

As you breathe in, imagine that you are taking in the earth's energy. Continue to breathe deeply and visualize the energy entering your body and filling you up. You should feel more grounded and connected to the earth with each breath. Feel the earth's energy entering your body and filling you with strength and stability. Open your eyes and continue with your readings when you feel well grounded.

Ways to Prepare Your Mind

If you're interested in developing your mediumship skills, you need to prepare your mind. It's a good idea to keep an open mind and be open to the possibility of receiving messages from beyond. However, it's also crucial to be mindful of your thoughts and emotions. These negative emotions will block you from receiving messages if you feel doubtful, scared, or anxious. Finding a balance between being open-minded and maintaining positive thoughts is essential. There are a few things you can do to prepare your mind for a reading:

1. Meditation

Suppose you're interested in developing your mediumship skills. In that case, one of the best things you can do is learn how to meditate. It can help to still your mind and open your consciousness, making it easier to receive psychic impressions from the spirit world. There are many different ways to meditate, so experiment until you find a method that works for you.

Some people prefer to sit or lie in a quiet place, focusing on their breath and letting their thoughts come and go without judgment. Others prefer to focus on a mantra or visualize a white light surrounding them. There is no right or wrong way to meditate. Find a practice that helps you to relax and open your mind. Regular meditation can help you to develop your mediumistic abilities and strengthen your connection to the spirit world.

2. Visualization

Visualization is one of the best ways to prepare your mind for mediumship. It is the process of creating mental images in your mind to achieve a specific goal. When you visualize, you use your imagination to create an image of what you want to happen. For example, if you want to communicate with a loved one who has passed away, you would visualize the two of you talking and sharing memories. The more realistic and detailed the image, the better.

The goal is to create a clear picture in your mind so that when you enter into mediumship, you'll be able to see and hear your loved one more clearly. Visualization has many other benefits, such as reducing stress and increasing your overall well-being. If you are new to visualization, start practicing daily for a few minutes. As you become more comfortable with the practice, you can increase the time you spend visualizing.

3. Affirmations

If you're interested in developing your mediumship skills, you can do a few things to prepare your mind. One of the most important is to practice affirmations. This involves repeating positive statements about your ability to connect with the other side. For example, you might say, "I am a gifted medium who can communicate with those who have passed on." By regularly repeating these affirmations, you'll begin to increase your self-confidence and belief in your abilities. This will make it easier for you to relax and open yourself up to the spirit world.

In addition to affirmations, another helpful way to prepare your mind for mediumship is to meditate while affirming positive thoughts. This will help you to still your thoughts and achieve a state of inner peace. When you can quieten your mind, it will be easier to receive messages from the other side. Be open-minded and receptive to the possibility of communicating with spirits. If you approach mediumship with skepticism or doubt, it will be more difficult to receive clear messages. Following these simple tips can set you up for success as a medium.

4. Prayer

Praying is one of the most crucial things you can do to prepare your mind for mediumship. Prayer quiets the mind and clears away any distracting thoughts. It also helps to open the heart, making it more receptive to communication from the Spirits. When praying, imagine yourself surrounded by light. Picture the light expanding until it fills your entire being. Sense the light infusing you with peace, love, and strength. Let go of all your fears and doubts, and allow yourself to be filled with the light of Spirit. As you do so, you'll find it easier to quieten your mind and open your heart to communication from the other side.

5. Connecting with Nature

Connecting with nature is one of the most effective ways to get into the right mindset. Spend time surrounded by plants and trees, and take in the beauty of the natural world. This will help you to quiet your mind and focus your thoughts. You might also want to try meditating or doing some deep-breathing exercises. These activities will help still your mind and allow you to receive guidance from the other side. Remember, the key is to relax and allow yourself to be open to the experience. With a little practice, you'll be surprised at what you're able to accomplish.

6. Keeping an Open Mind

When getting your mind ready for mediumship, it is vital to have an open perspective. Throughout history, many people have been skeptical of mediumship and the ability to communicate with the dead. However, remember that mediumship is a natural ability that we all possess. Just as we can use our five senses to interact with the physical world, we can also use our sixth sense to interact with the spiritual world. With an open mind, you'll be able to more easily receive messages from your loved ones who have passed on. In addition, you'll also be more receptive to messages from your spirit guide. Keep an open mind, and you'll be well on your way to becoming a successful medium.

7. Trusting Your Intuition

To prepare your mind for the experience, learn to trust your intuition. Intuition is our inner guidance system and is often the first step in receiving psychic information. To develop it, it's crucial to quiet your mind and get in touch with your feelings. Meditation can be a helpful tool for this, but simply taking some time each day to focus on your breath can also be helpful. It's also essential to pay attention to the messages you receive from your body. Our bodies often give us information about people and situations before our minds do. By learning to trust your intuition, you'll open yourself up to a new world of psychic experiences.

8. Yoga

You've probably heard of yoga before, but did you know that it can also be used to prepare your mind for mediumship? It is an ancient practice that involves physical, mental, and spiritual disciplines. The physical aspect of yoga involves stretching and strengthening the body. In contrast, the mental and spiritual aspects involve breathwork and meditation. By focusing on the breath and clearing the mind of all other thoughts, yoga can help to still the mind and create a sense of inner peace. This state of mind is ideal for mediumship as it makes connecting with the spirit world easier. In addition, it can also help to develop psychic abilities and expand your consciousness. So if you're looking for a way to prepare your mind for mediumship, yoga might be the perfect option for you.

When engaging in mediumship, it is critical to be properly grounded and have your mind focused on the task at hand. Grounding yourself will help to protect you from outside influences and clear your mind of any unwanted thoughts or distractions. You can ground yourself by visualizing roots growing from your feet and anchoring you to the earth. Once you are grounded, prepare your mind for the session. This can be done through meditation or visualization exercises. It is also crucial to take some time to connect with nature. Spend a few minutes focusing on your breath and taking in the peace and beauty of your surroundings. By taking these steps, you'll receive accurate messages during your session and be better able to focus.

Chapter 4: How to Recognize Energy

Have you ever walked into a room and felt an instant connection or disconnection with the people in it? Have you ever been able to sense the energy of a person or place just by being near it? If so, then you may have already experienced the act of sensing energy.

Mediums can open themselves up to seeing and communicating with the spirit world.
https://www.pexels.com/photo/woman-doing-a-card-reading-8770834/

In mediumship, recognizing and understanding the energy around you can be extremely helpful when it comes to discerning the difference between a deceased loved one and a lower-vibrational entity. It can also help you understand the messages you receive. The energy of a person or place can tell you a lot about what they are thinking or feeling at any given moment.

There are many different ways to sense energy. Some people are more naturally attuned to sensing energy than others, but with a little practice, anyone can learn how to do it. This chapter will teach you how to visualize and sense energy on your own and with others. It will also provide you with some exercises you can practice to develop your ability to sense energy.

How to Visualize and Sense Energy

Visualizing and sensing energy are two important skills for anyone interested in mediumship. Through visualization, mediums can open themselves up to seeing and communicating with the spirit world. By sensing energy, mediums can interpret the emotions and thoughts of spirits. These abilities require practice and concentration, but they can be developed with time and patience. Sensing energy is a skill that takes time and practice to develop. The more you practice, the better you'll become at it. Here are some tips to help you develop your ability to visualize and sense energy:

1. Relax and Open Your Mind

The ability to see and feel energy is a skill that anyone can learn. However, it does take some practice to develop this ability. The first step is to relax and clear your mind. It is crucial to be in a state of relaxation to sense energy. Once you are relaxed, start to focus on your breath. Take slow, deep breaths and allow your mind to become calm and still. Once you have reached a state of inner peace, start to visualize energy. See it swirling around you, filling the space with its bright light. Feel the energy flowing through your body, energizing and revitalizing you. With practice, you'll develop the ability to sense energy more clearly. Eventually, you'll be able to see and feel the energy all around you, anytime and anywhere.

2. Look for a Change in Your Environment

One way to tell if there is an energy change in your environment is to see if the space around you feels different. For example, if you walk into a room that feels heavy or dense, there may be negative energy. Alternatively, if a space feels light and airy, it may be because the energy is positive. Another way to sense energy is to *focus on your body*. If you suddenly feel tense or uncomfortable, it may be because negative energy is nearby. On the other hand, if you feel relaxed and at ease, it could be because the energy in your environment is positive.

3. Pay Attention to Your Physical Sensations

One way to become more attuned to energy is to pay attention to your physical sensations. For example, you might notice that you feel lighter when you are in the presence of positive energy and heavier or constricted when you are around negative energy. You might also notice changes in your breathing, heart rate, or tingling sensation. These are just some of the ways your body can respond to different kinds of energy. By paying attention to your physical sensations, you can begin to get a sense of the different energy types around you.

4. Notice How You Feel Emotionally and Mentally

You may not see energy, but you can most certainly feel it. Energy is everywhere, and it affects us in both subtle and profound ways. Learning how to visualize and sense energy can help us understand our own emotions and mental state, as well as the energies of others. When we pay attention to how we feel emotionally and mentally, we can begin to get a sense of the energy around us. Pay attention to your emotions and thoughts. If you feel angry or anxious for no reason, it could be because of an energetic imbalance. However, if you feel happy and peaceful, it may be because the energy around you is supportive. By paying attention to these signs, you can get a better sense of the energy in your environment.

6. Trust Your Intuition

Energy is all around us, but it can be hard to sense and visualize. Some people seem to have a natural ability to see and feel the energy, while others find it more difficult. However, there are some things that you can do to help yourself become more attuned to the energy around you. One of the most essential things is to trust your intuition. If you get a feeling or see something in your mind's eye, don't second-guess yourself – go with it. It's also helpful to spend time in nature, where you can feel the energy flow around you. And finally, don't be afraid to experiment. There are many different ways to sense and see energy, so try out different techniques until you find one that works. With a little practice, you'll be amazed at how much easier it is to connect with the world of energy that surrounds us all.

7. Practice, Practice, Practice!

Learning how to visualize and sense energy is a skill that takes time and practice to develop. The first step is to simply become aware of the energy around you. Start by focusing on objects in your environment and notice the energy they emit. Once you become more attuned to the energy around you, you can experiment with ways of manipulating it. For example, try holding your hands a few inches apart and focusing on the energy flow between them. Keep practicing until you develop a stronger sense of how energy works and how it can be used to improve your health and well-being.

Exercises for Sensing One's Energy

Energy is all around us. It's in the air we breathe, the food we eat, and the water we drink. It's also in the people we interact with and the places we visit. Our bodies are made up of energy, and our thoughts and emotions are also forms of energy. We constantly interact with energy, whether or not we are aware of it. One way to become more aware of it is to learn how to sense your energy field. This can be done through various methods, including meditation, visualization, and breathwork. By taking the time to sense your energy, you can become more attuned to the energy around you. Doing so can teach you how to better manage it and create a more positive and balanced life. Here are some exercises to help you get started:

1. The Ball of Light Exercise

You can learn to sense your energy even if you can't see it. One way to do this is through the "ball of light" exercise. First, find a comfortable place to sit or lie down. Close your eyes and take a few deep breaths. Then, imagine a ball of light inside your chest. It can be any color or size that you choose. Spend a few minutes focusing on the ball of light, and pay attention to any sensations that you feel in your body. You may feel warmth, tingling, or pulsing. The more you focus on the ball of light, the stronger these sensations will become. With practice, you'll be able to sense your energy more and more clearly.

2. The Rope Exercise

We're all empathic beings, capable of sensing the energy of those around us. And while it's a skill that can be useful in many situations, it can also be overwhelming if we're not used to it. One way to start learning how to control your ability to sense energy is by doing the rope exercise.

The rope exercise is simple. Find a partner and stand facing each other, about an arm's length apart. Take turns holding one end of a rope while your partner holds the other. Then, try to communicate your energy to your partner through the rope without speaking. Focus on sending calm or happy energy, and see if they can receive it. You may be surprised at how well it works! With practice, you'll be able to better control your abilities and use them in more helpful ways rather than overwhelming.

3. The Scanning Exercise

The scanning exercise is an easy way to train yourself to be more aware of your energy. To begin, find a comfortable place to sit or lie down. Close your eyes and take a few deep breaths, allowing your body to relax. Once you feel calm, focus your attention on your breath. Inhale deeply, and then exhale slowly. As you breathe, imagine you are drawing in energy from the air around you. This energy will fill your body, infusing every cell with vitality.

Once you feel filled with energy, begin to scan your body from head to toe. Notice how this energy feels as it flows through you. Pay attention to any areas where the energy feels particularly strong or weak. With practice, you'll develop a greater sensitivity to the flow of energy within your own body. This exercise can be done anywhere, at any time, making it easy to cultivate your ability to sense energy. By learning to sense your energy, you'll be better positioned to detect and understand the energy of others.

4. The Ray of Light Exercise

We are all energy beings and constantly interact with the energy around us. Just like we tune into different channels on a TV, we can tune into different energy frequencies. When we tune into a high frequency, we feel good. We feel happy, joyful, and at ease. When we tune into a low frequency, we feel bad. We feel angry, sad, and anxious. Learning to sense energy can help us to avoid negative people and situations and attract more of what we want into our lives.

The Ray of Light exercise is one method to practice sensing energy. First, find a comfortable place to sit or lie down. Close your eyes and take a few deep breaths. Then imagine a ray of light shining down from the sky and hitting you in the center of your forehead. The light will enter your body and fill you with positive energy. As you breathe in, feel the light expanding throughout your body. Fill your entire being with the light until you radiate positive energy. Now open your eyes and notice how you feel.

You should feel lighter, brighter, and more at peace. With practice, you'll be able to sense energy anywhere, anytime!

5. The Crystal Ball Exercise

One of the best ways to get in touch with your energy is to do the crystal ball exercise. This exercise is simple and only takes a few minutes. To begin, sit comfortably and hold a crystal ball in your hands. Close your eyes and take a few deep breaths. Imagine that your breath is filling the crystal ball with light as you breathe. Once the ball is filled up, imagine it emanating from the center and moving outward in all directions. Continue to breathe deeply and focus on the light until you feel yourself becoming calm and relaxed.

Now, imagine that you are looking into the crystal ball and that it is showing you images of your energy. Observe the color, shape, and movement of the energy in the ball. Spend a few minutes observing your energy before opening your eyes. When you have finished, take a few deep breaths and write down what you saw in the crystal ball. This exercise is a great way to get in touch with your energy and learn more about how it affects your everyday life.

6. The Grounding Exercise

We must learn how to sense and connect with our energy to live healthy, happy lives. The grounding exercise is one way to help improve your focus. To begin, find a comfortable place to sit or stand. Close your eyes and take a few deep breaths. As you inhale, imagine roots growing down from your feet into the earth. With each exhale, feel yourself becoming more rooted and grounded.

Allow yourself to sink deeply into the earth. Imagine its energy coming up through your roots and into your body. Breathe in this nourishing energy and let it fill you up. When you're ready, open your eyes and take a few minutes to notice how you feel. You should feel more connected to the earth and more centered within yourself. With practice, you'll be able to access this feeling anytime, anywhere.

7. The Centering Exercise

Most people are unaware of the energy they exude. We go about our days not sensing the effect we have on those around us. However, this energy is very real and can be harnessed to create positive outcomes in our lives. You can get in touch with your energy by doing the centering exercise. Start by closing your eyes and taking a few deep breaths. Then, focus on your hands and imagine a white light emanating from them. This light represents your energy.

Now, bring your hands slowly up to your chest and imagine the light entering your heart space. As you do this, you should feel a sense of calm and relaxation wash over you. Continue to breathe deeply and focus on the light until you feel fully centered. This exercise can be done anytime you need to connect with your energy and center yourself.

Sensing Others' Energy

Many experts believe that we are all connected by an invisible energy field. This field is often referred to as the "aura." Some people can see the aura, while others can sense it. Sensing the aura of others is sometimes called "auric sensing." There are many different ways to sense someone else's energy. For some people, it may be a physical feeling, like warmth or tingling in the body. Others may get a mental or emotional sense of the person's energy. And some people may see colors or shapes around the person.

If you think you may be sensing other people's energy, you can do a few things to develop your ability. With practice, you may find that you're able to sense the energy of others more clearly. And who knows? You may even discover that you have a hidden talent for auric sensing. Here are a few things you can do to develop your ability to sense others' energy:

1. The Mirror Exercise

We are all walking around with our energy field or aura. You may not be able to see it, but you can feel it. When you walk into a room, you can sense the energy of the people around you. Some people have calm, soothing energy, while others have high energy, which is almost overwhelming. Have you ever walked into a room and felt instantly uncomfortable? That is because you were picking up on the negative energy of the people around you.

Fortunately, there is a way to protect yourself from negative energy and even start to influence the energy of the people around you. It's called the mirror exercise, and it is a simple but powerful tool for sensing and managing energy. The exercise is exactly what it sounds like - you stand in front of a mirror and imagine your aura reflecting on you. As you look at your reflection, imagine your aura is strong and bright. Visualize your energy being so strong that it fills up the entire mirror. Now, imagine that the people around you are reflecting their energy field. See their auras filling up the space around them. Finally, imagine that your aura is so powerful that it starts to influence the energy of the people around you, making them calmer and more positive.

The mirror exercise is a great way to get in touch with your energy field and start to manage the energy of the people around you. Give it a try next time you walk into a room full of people and see how it makes you feel.

2. The Empathy Exercise

By becoming more attuned to the energy around us, we can learn to protect our positive energy and prevent it from being drained. That's what the empathy exercise is all about. The first step is finding a quiet place to relax and clear your mind. Once you're calm, start paying attention to the people around you. Notice how their energy makes you feel. Are you feeling happy and upbeat, or are you feeling tired and down?

If you start to feel negative after being around someone, it's a good sign that their energy is negatively affecting you. In this case, it's best to try to avoid them. However, if you're drawn to someone's positive energy, then, by all means, talk to them! By practicing this exercise, you can become more attuned to the energies around you and learn to protect your positive energy.

3. The Cord-Cutting Exercise

Negative energy can be contagious, but so can positive energy. The key is to surround yourself with people who have positive energy and avoid those who drain you. That's where the cord-cutting exercise comes in. This exercise is designed to help you break free from the negative energy of others so that you can surround yourself with positive people.

To perform the cord-cutting exercise, imagine a bright white light surrounding you. This light is your protection from negative energy. Now, imagine that you are surrounded by people who drain your energy. See their negative energy as dark cords attached to you and draining you. Now, use your imagination to cut these cords. See the cords being cut and falling away from you. As you do that, you'll feel your energy shift and change. You'll feel lighter and more positive. Finally, imagine that you are surrounded by people who have positive energy. See their bright light shining around you. Their positive energy fills you up and makes you happy and healthy.

The cord-cutting exercise is a great way to break free from the negative energy of others and surround yourself with positive people. Give it a try and see how it makes you feel.

By learning to sense and manage energy, you can protect yourself from negative energy and even start to influence the people around you. These exercises are just a starting point. The more you practice, the better you'll become at managing your energy and that of others. So don't be afraid to experiment and see what works best for you. And remember, the more positive energy you put into the world, the more you'll get in return!

Chapter 5: Developing Clairvoyance and Other Clairs

Have you ever wished you could see into the future? Hear what someone is thinking? Or just know things you never did before? If so, then you may be interested in developing your mediumship skills.

Clairvoyance is the ability to see spirits.
https://www.pexels.com/photo/hands-over-fortune-telling-crystal-ball-7179800/

Mediumship is the ability to communicate with the spirits of those who have passed on; it is a skill anyone can learn. There are different ways to develop your mediumship skills. Still, one of the most crucial things is learning to use your clairvoyance, clairaudience, clairsentience, and Claircognizance. This chapter will explore what each of these clairs entails and how you can develop them. By the end of this chapter, you'll have plenty of tools and knowledge to use your mediumship skills in everyday life!

The Four Clairs

The Four Clairs are four ways we can receive information from the spiritual realm. Clairvoyance is the ability to see spirits, clairaudience is the ability to hear them, clairsentience is the ability to feel or sense them, and Claircognizance is the ability to know and understand them. We all have these abilities, but some are more attuned to one or two of them. For example, you may be a clairvoyant who sees images or symbols when you meditate or a clairaudient who hears voices or music. Or you may be a clairsentient who feels energy or emotions or a claircognizant who just knows things. These are all valid ways to receive information from spirits, and there is no right or wrong way to do it. The vital thing is to be open to whatever form of communication comes through for you. Let's explore each of the four clairs in more depth.

Clairvoyance
(What to Expect When You're Clairvoyant)

Clairvoyance is the ability to see beyond the five physical senses. Clairvoyant people may see colors and shapes representing people, events, or messages from the other side. Clairvoyance is often associated with psychic ability, but it is important to note that not all psychics are clairvoyant. Some clairvoyants may also have other abilities, such as clairaudience (clear hearing) or clairsentience (clear feeling). Clairvoyant people may see images in their mind's eye, or they may see actual physical objects. Some people report seeing auras around people, while others say they see symbols or flashes of light. This ability can be helpful in many areas of life, from careers to relationships. Many resources are available to help you develop and understand your gift if you think you may be clairvoyant. The most important thing is to trust your intuition and follow your heart.

How to Develop Clairvoyance

Everyone has clairvoyant abilities, but most people are unaware of them or do not know how to develop them. There are many ways to develop clairvoyance, but the most crucial thing is to have an open mind and be willing to explore your abilities.

One way to develop clairvoyance is through intuition. Intuition is an inner knowing that comes from the subconscious mind. We all have intuition, but many of us do not listen to it. To develop your intuition, start by paying attention to your gut feelings. If you get a feeling about something, take some time to investigate it further. You may be surprised at what you find.

Another way to develop clairvoyance is through synchronicities. Synchronicities are meaningful coincidences that cannot be explained by logic or chance. They often occur when we think about someone or something, and they suddenly appear in our lives. For example, you may be thinking about a friend and then run into them at the grocery store. These coincidences are a sign that the universe is trying to get our attention. Pay attention to them and see where they lead you.

Finally, another way to develop clairvoyance is through visions. Visions are glimpses of the future that come to us in our dreams or meditation. To interpret your visions, keep a dream journal and write down any strange or significant dreams you have. You may also want to try meditation or guided visualization exercises. As you practice accessing your psychic abilities, you'll see more clearly in the spiritual realm.

Tips to Improve Clairvoyance

If you are interested in improving your clairvoyant abilities, you can do a few things to speed up the process.

- **Practice Daily:** The more you practice using your abilities, the stronger they will become. Spend some time practicing visualization exercises or working with a psychic medium each day.
- **Get a Reading:** A professional psychic reading can give you some insight into your abilities and what you should be working on.
- **Join a Development Circle:** Many development circles or groups meet regularly to help people develop their abilities. This is a great way to meet other like-minded people and learn from more experienced psychics.

- **Keep a Journal:** Journaling is a great way to track your progress and document your experiences. Write down any dreams, visions, or synchronicities you have.

Clairaudience
(What to Expect When You're Clairaudient)

Clairaudience is the ability to hear spirit. This can manifest in many ways, from hearing an inner voice guiding you to hearing sounds like music or laughter. You may even receive messages from Spirit through words or phrases. Clairaudience is often one of the first psychic abilities to develop, and it's a skill that can be used in many different ways. For example, you can use clairaudience to communicate with your Spirit Guides to receive guidance from them on your life path. You can also use clairaudience to connect with loved ones who have passed on and to receive messages from them.

Clairaudience in Everyday Life

Clairaudience can manifest in several ways, from hearing the sounds of nature to receiving messages from the other side. As you develop your clairaudient abilities, you may start to notice that you can more easily remember your dreams. You may also find that you are drawn to certain sounds, such as the sound of running water or birdsong. Clairaudience can also be used to tune into your higher self. By listening for guidance from within, you can begin to make choices that are in alignment with your true desires. With practice, clairaudience can be a powerful tool for accessing inner wisdom and guidance.

How to Develop Clairaudience

Clairaudience is the ability to hear voices and sounds that are not audible to the human ear. These sounds can come from either the spirit world or your higher self. Suppose you are interested in developing this ability. In that case, you can do a few things to open yourself up to the possibility. First, it is important to have an open mind and be receptive to the idea that you may be able to hear things beyond the physical world. Second, try practicing with a friend or medium already attuned to clairaudience. This will help you become more comfortable with the experience.

Finally, try automatic writing. This technique allows your hand to move freely across a sheet of paper without consciously thinking about what you are writing. The words that come through may not make immediate sense, but over time, you may start to see patterns and messages meant for you. Clairaudience is a fascinating ability that can help you connect with the unseen world around you. You may be surprised at what you can hear with a little practice.

Tips for Improving Clairaudience

- **Meditation:** Meditation is a great way to quieten the mind down and open it up to the possibility of hearing the spirit.
- **Relaxation:** Be relaxed when you are trying to develop your clairaudient abilities. Try to find a quiet place where you will not be interrupted.
- **Visualization:** Visualization can be helpful when you are trying to hear spirit. Picturing yourself in a peaceful place, surrounded by nature, can help you attune to the frequency of the spirit.
- **Get in Touch with Your Emotions:** Our emotions are closely linked to our ability to hear spirits. By getting in touch with your feelings, you can start to become more attuned to the messages coming through.
- **Visualize What You Want to Hear:** If you are looking for guidance from your Spirit Guides, try to visualize what you would like to hear. This can help to open up the channel of communication.

Clairsentience
(What to Expect When You're Clairsentient)

Being clairsentient means that you experience psychic impressions through your feelings. In other words, you "know" things on a gut level, even if you can't explain how you know them. Clairsentience is one of the most common forms of psychic ability and is also one of the easiest to develop. As you open yourself up to your psychic abilities, you may find that your gut feelings become stronger and more accurate. With practice, you can learn to use your clairsentience to guide you in all areas of your life.

Clairsentience in Everyday Life

Clairsentient individuals often report having empathic abilities, meaning they can sense the emotions of others. They may also experience strong intuitions or "gut feelings" about people and situations. In addition, clairsentients often notice significant coincidences, or what is known as "synchronicity." While some people may dismiss these experiences as mere coincidence, clairsentients know they are receiving guidance from a higher source. They can navigate the world more intuitively by attuning to their inner feelings.

How to Develop Clairsentience

Most people are familiar with the five senses, but did you know that there is a sixth sense? This sense, known as clairsentience, refers to the ability to receive information from beyond the physical world. While some people are born with this ability, it is also possible to develop clairsentience through spiritual practice. Here are three ways to get started:

Connecting with Your Emotions: Clairsentience is often described as an "empathic" ability, meaning that those who can access this sense are very in tune with their emotions. If you want to develop your clairsentience, start by spending time getting in touch with your feelings. Notice what makes you feel good and what makes you feel bad. Pay attention to your intuition, and don't be afraid to trust your gut feeling.

Learning How to Meditate: Meditation is an excellent way to quiet the mind and focus on the present moment. When you meditate, you create a space for stillness and clarity. As you become more comfortable with meditation, you may start to notice intuitive insights emerging from the silence. These insights can be a valuable form of guidance from the Higher Self or Spirit Guides.

Practicing Grounding and Centering: To receive psychic information, it is important to be grounded and centered. This means that you are present in your body and aware of your surroundings. You can ground yourself by visualizing roots growing from your feet and anchoring you into the earth. To center yourself, focus on your breath, and let go of any thoughts or distractions. With practice, you'll become better at receiving clear and accurate information from the spiritual realm.

Tips for Improving Clairsentience

If you're interested in developing your clairsentience, there are a few things you can do to help the process along:

- **Commit to Exploring Your Psychic Ability Regularly:** The more you work with your clairsentience, the stronger it will become. To see results, it is important to be consistent with your practice. Set aside some time each day to focus on developing your psychic ability.

- **Be Open to All Forms of Communication:** Clairsentience is often described as a gut feeling, but it can also manifest in other ways. You may receive information through dreams, symbols, or even physical sensations. Pay attention to how you receive information and be open to all forms of communication from the spiritual realm.
- **Practice Discerning between Your Thoughts and Psychic Information:** It can be tricky to distinguish between your thoughts and psychic impressions. A good way to tell the difference is to ask yourself if the information you are receiving is based on fear or love. If the answer is fear, the information is likely coming from your mind. However, if the answer is love, it is more likely that the information is coming from a higher source.
- **Let Go of Expectations:** When you are first starting, it is important to let go of any expectations you have about the process. Psychic ability is a subtle sense, and it may take some time to get in touch with your clairsentient abilities. Be patient and trust that the information you need will be revealed in due time.

Claircognizance
(What to Expect When You're Claircognizant)

Claircognizance is a type of extrasensory perception that refers to the ability to know things without prior knowledge or understanding. This ability is often described as a "sixth sense" or "gut feeling," and it can be used to obtain information about people, places, events, or objects. Claircognizance differs from other forms of ESP, such as clairvoyance and clairaudience, in that it does not involve seeing or hearing things that are not ordinarily available to the senses. Instead, claircognizant individuals simply know things that they could not possibly know through normal means.

This form of extrasensory perception allows access to information unavailable through the five senses. It's also known as "clear knowing" or "inner knowing." Claircognizance often manifests as a strong inner knowing or hunch about something. It's a sense that goes beyond what you can see, hear, taste, smell, or touch. Although there is no scientific evidence to support the existence of Claircognizance, many people believe that this ability is real and that it can be harnessed to obtain valuable information.

Claircognizance in Everyday Life

Claircognizance can be used in various ways in everyday life. For example, you might receive divine guidance through Claircognizance. You might also use your intuition to make decisions based on your inner knowledge. Claircognizant people often become successful business owners, stockbrokers, and police officers because they know how to listen to their gut feelings and follow their instincts.

Claircognizance often manifests as a "gut feeling" about someone or something. You just know that something is true, even though there's no logical reason to feel that way. Claircognizance can be a very useful tool in everyday life. For example, you might use it to:

- **Make Decisions:** If you're trying to decide whether or not to take a new job, for example, you may get a claircognizant sense of whether or not it's the right choice for you.
- **Get Guidance:** Many people like to ask their claircognizant selves for advice on important decisions. All you need to do is focus on your question and then let the answer come to you.
- **Sense Danger:** If you're walking down a dark alley and suddenly get a strong sense that you're in danger, your Claircognizance is trying to warn you. Listen to your intuition and get out of there!

Claircognizance is just one of many different psychic abilities. Still, it's one that we can all use in our everyday lives if we learn how to listen to our intuition.

How to Develop Claircognizance

If you're interested in developing your claircognizant abilities, there are several things you can do to nurture this process. Meditation is one way to calm the mind and open yourself up to receiving inner guidance. You can also practice visualization exercises and ask for signs from the universe about a particular decision you're trying to make. Pay attention to your dreams, as they can also provide helpful guidance. As you begin to trust your inner knowing, you'll start to notice Claircognizance becoming a more regular part of your life. Claircognizance is a powerful gift that can help you live a more intuitive and fulfilling life.

Tips for Improving Claircognizance

If you want to improve your Claircognizance, there are a few things you can do:

- **Be Willing to Receive:** For Claircognizance to work, you must be willing to receive information from your higher self. If you're not open to the idea of inner guidance, you'll likely block any information that comes through.
- **Get Comfortable with Silence:** One of the best ways to open yourself up to claircognizant abilities is to get comfortable with silence. Meditation and mindfulness are excellent ways to quieten the mind and connect with your inner knowing.
- **Trust Your Intuition:** When you receive a hunch or feeling about something, trust it. The more you trust your intuition, the stronger your claircognizant abilities will become.
- **Be Patient:** Claircognizance is a process that takes time and patience. Don't expect to become an expert overnight. Trust that the information will come when you're ready to receive it.
- **Listen to Your Inner Voice:** We all have an inner voice that speaks to us. This is the voice of our higher selves. Pay attention to your inner voice and trust that it is guiding you in the right direction.
- **Follow Your Heart:** Our hearts are often wiser than our minds. If you're struggling to make a decision, follow your heart. It will usually lead you in the right direction.

The four main clairs are:
- Clairvoyance (seeing images),
- Clairaudience (hearing sounds),
- Clairsentience (recognizing feelings)
- Claircognizance (knowing).

We all have one or more of these skills, but they might be dormant, and we need to tap into them. In mediumship, clairvoyance is seeing images of the deceased or other beings in the spirit world. Clairaudience is hearing sounds, such as the voice of the deceased or other beings in the spirit world. Clairsentience recognizes feelings, such as the emotions of the deceased or other beings in the spirit world. Claircognizance knows things without having any physical evidence or logical explanation for why you do.

You can do several things to develop your Clair abilities, such as meditating, practicing visualization exercises, and asking for signs from the universe. You can also improve your clairs by getting comfortable with silence, trusting your intuition, and being patient. Remember to listen to your inner voice and follow your heart. The more you trust these abilities, the more they will become a part of your everyday life.

Chapter 6: Spirit Channeling 101

Have you ever wanted to connect with a loved one who has passed away? Or perhaps you're curious about your roots and want to connect with your ancestors? If so, you may be interested in learning about spirit channeling. Spirit channeling is a practice that allows you to connect with the spirits of deceased loved ones or ancestors. It's similar to mediumship, but there are some key differences. In this chapter, we'll explore what spirit channeling is, how it's different from mediumship, and how to do it.

Many different techniques can be used to channel spirits, but one of the most crucial things is to create a space where you feel safe.
https://www.pexels.com/photo/playing-cards-laid-down-on-a-table-top-with-velvet-cover-8770810/

Spirit Channeling

Many people are fascinated by the idea of spirit channeling, where a person becomes a medium for communicating messages from beyond the physical world. While some people may be skeptical of this practice, there is no doubt that it has been practiced for centuries in cultures worldwide. The ancient Egyptians, for example, believed that their Pharaohs were channels to the gods, and many indigenous peoples believed their shamans could communicate with spirits.

Some people believe that anyone can learn to channel spirits. In contrast, others believe it is a gift only certain people possess. Many different techniques can be used to channel spirits, but one of the most crucial things is to create a space where you feel safe and comfortable. This may mean lighting candles or incense or playing soothing music. Once you have created your space, you can begin to clear your mind and focus on your breath. It may take some time to reach a state of deep relaxation, but once you do, you may find that you can channel messages from beyond the physical world.

Mediumship vs. Spirit Channeling

When it comes to connecting with the world beyond, there are two main approaches that people take: mediumship and spirit channeling. Both of these practices can be used to communicate with spirits, but there are some key distinctions between them.

Although "mediumship" and "spirit channeling" are often used interchangeably, they refer to two different things. Mediumship is the ability to communicate with spirits who have passed on to the other side, while spirit channeling is the act of allowing a spirit to temporarily possess your body to communicate with the living. Channeling generally implies that the medium is not in control of the situation and that they are simply providing a vessel for the spirit to use.

Mediumship can be used for a variety of purposes, such as providing comfort to the bereaved or delivering messages from beyond the grave. Spirit channeling, on the other hand, is often used to gain insights or knowledge that would otherwise be unavailable. Channeled messages can come from various sources, including departed loved ones, guardian angels, or even higher beings such as Jesus or Buddha. Ultimately, whether you're seeking comfort or wisdom, both mediumship and spirit channeling can provide valuable insights into the afterlife.

Both mediumship and spirit channeling can provide information and guidance from the other side. However, each approach has its benefits and drawbacks. Mediumship may be more effective for communicating specific messages, while channeling may be better for receiving general information. Ultimately, it is up to the individual to decide which approach is best for them.

Spirit Channeling in Shamanism

Shamanism is an ancient spiritual practice involving communing with the spirit to heal the physical world. Central to shamanism is the belief that everything in the universe is connected and that disease or disharmony occurs when this connection is broken. Shamans enter into trances to journey to the spirit realm and repair these broken connections. This practice is known as "spirit channeling."

To journey to the spirit realm, shamans use various methods, such as drumming, dancing, singing, and visualization. Once they have entered into a trance state, they will often receive guidance from helpful spirits through symbols or images. By interpreting these messages, shamans can identify the root cause of a problem and take steps to correct it. In this way, spirit channeling can be a powerful tool for healing physical ills and restoring balance to the natural world.

Spirit Channeling in Voodoo

Voodoo is an Afro-Caribbean religious tradition that combines elements of West African Vodun, Catholicism, and Native American traditions. One of the most unique aspects of Voodoo is spirit channeling. This is a practice where a medium goes into a trance and allows a spirit to take over their body to communicate with the living.

Spirit channeling is said to be a very powerful experience, both for the person who is channeling and for those who are witnessing it. The spirit being channeled is said to be able to impart wisdom and knowledge they have gained in the afterlife, and they can also offer guidance and advice. For the person doing the channeling, it can be a deeply moving experience that helps them connect with their spirituality.

If you are interested in experiencing spirit channeling, you should seek out a reputable Voodoo priest or priestess. They will help you prepare for the experience and create a safe space for you to journey into the spirit world.

Spirit Channeling in Spiritualism

Spirit channeling is a practice that has been used for centuries by many different cultures. The basic idea is that a spirit world exists beyond our physical world and can communicate with these spirits. There are many ways to channel spirits, but the most common method is through mediumship. This involves going into a trance-like state and allowing the spirit to take control of your body and voice to communicate with the living.

Spiritualism is a religion where people believe in the existence of a spirit world and the ability to communicate with those who have passed on. Many spiritualists believe that we can all learn from the wisdom of the spirits and that they can help us better navigate our lives. Spirit channeling is one of the main ways spiritualists connect with the spirit world and is an essential part of their belief system.

Many resources are available online and in libraries, if you are interested in learning more about spiritualism or spirit channeling. There are also many spiritualist churches around the world where you can meet other like-minded people and explore this fascinating belief system.

The Trance State

All of these traditions have one thing in common: the trance state. This is a natural state of consciousness that we all experience every day. It is the state between wakefulness and sleep and a very powerful state for spirit channeling. To channel spirits, you must first enter into a trance state.

There are many ways to induce a trance state, but the most common method is through meditation. Meditation is a practice that allows you to focus your mind and achieve a state of deep relaxation. Once you reach this state, your conscious mind will be quiet, and you'll be more open to receiving messages from the spirit world. There are many different types of meditation, so find a method that works for you. If you are new to meditation, many resources are available online and in libraries. Once you have learned how to meditate, you can begin to practice spirit channeling.

Another way to enter into a trance state is through hypnosis. Hypnosis is a state of deep relaxation induced by another person. The person hypnotizing you'll guide you into a trance state and help you focus your mind. Once in a trance, you'll be more open to receiving messages from the spirit world. This method is often used by mediums who are trying to channel spirits.

Whether Voodoo, Shamanism, or Spiritualism, channeling always starts with the practitioner going into a trance state. This could be done through meditation, hypnosis, or any other method that works for the individual. Entering this trance state is a necessary step in communicating with the beyond. After entering a trance, you'll be more open to receiving messages from the spirit world. These messages can come in the form of thoughts, feelings, or images. Remember that not all messages will make sense to you, but trust that the message is coming from a place of love and wisdom. Allow the message to guide you, and trust that it is for your highest good.

Channeling Your Ancestors

Maybe you have heard of people channeling their ancestors before, but what does that mean exactly? Channeling is when an individual goes into a trance-like state and becomes possessed by the spirit of another. This can happen spontaneously or through specific techniques, such as meditation or chanting.

Those who practice ancestor worship believe that our ancestors are around us, even after they have passed on. They can offer guidance and protection, and staying in communication with them is vital. Channeling is one way to do this.

You open yourself to their knowledge and wisdom when you channel your ancestors. You may receive messages about your personal life, or they may offer advice about important decisions you need to make. You may even find yourself speaking in a different language or with a different accent.

Ancestor worship is an ancient practice that is still practiced today in many cultures around the world. If you are interested in channeling your ancestors, here are a few things you can do to get started:

1. Investigating Your Lineage

Have you ever wondered about your ancestors? Who were they? Where did they come from? What were their lives like? If you have questions about your lineage, consider spirit channeling as a way to investigate your ancestry. It can help you communicate with the spirit world to gain information about a person's past. This information can provide insights into your family history and help you to connect with your ancestors on a deeper level.

If you're interested in exploring your lineage through spirit channeling, you should keep a few things in mind. First, finding a reputable medium with experience communicating with the departed is crucial. Second, be open to receiving whatever information comes through, even if it isn't what you expected or hoped for. And finally, trust your intuition. If something doesn't feel right, don't hesitate to ask follow-up questions or request clarification. By following these guidelines, you can ensure that your experience is both safe and insightful.

2. Going into a Trance State

Spirit channeling your ancestors can be a powerful experience. Entering into a trance state is a crucial step here. This can be done through meditation, breathing exercises, or even sleep. Once you're in a trance state, focus your intention on contacting your ancestors. You may want to say their names out loud or visualize them in your mind. Then, simply open yourself up to receive any messages they may have for you. Remember that not all messages will come through clearly. Sometimes, you may only receive snippets of information or vague impressions. However, with practice, you should be able to receive messages that are clearer and more concise.

3. Connecting with an Ancestor

When trying to connect with an ancestor, there are a few things you can do to prepare. First, create a peaceful and comfortable space where you won't be disturbed. You might want to light some candles or incense or play soothing music. Next, focus your attention on your breath and allow yourself to relax. Once you're feeling calm and centered, begin to visualize the ancestor or loved one you wish to connect with. As you do so, imagine a bright white light surrounding you and filling the room. Picture the light merging with your energy until you feel locked into place.

Now, simply ask the ancestor or loved one for guidance. Allow whatever comes into your mind to flow freely without judgment. If you don't receive an answer immediately, that's okay – just be patient and keep an open mind. You may find that Spirit Channeling your ancestors can provide valuable insights and guidance on your life journey.

4. Receiving Messages

Although our ancestors are no longer with us in physical form, they can still offer guidance and support from the spirit world. One way to connect with them is through a technique where you open yourself up to receive messages. It can be done alone or with the help of a medium. The key is to relax and allow the messages to come through. You may hear them as a voice in your head, or you may receive visual images or feelings. Trust your intuition and go with whatever comes up. Keep an open mind, and don't be afraid to ask questions. Remember, your ancestors want to help you and will only give you helpful information.

5. Interpreting Messages

Channeling is a broadly defined term that can refer to any type of communication with spirits. This includes communicating with deceased loved ones, guides, angels, and other non-physical beings. Channeling can take many different forms, from hearing voices in your head to seeing visions in your mind's eye. However, the most important thing is to be open to receiving messages from the other side. Once you've established a connection, it's crucial to interpret the meaning of the message you've received. This can often be done using intuition or consulting with a trusted psychic or medium. With a little practice, you'll be surprised at how easy it is to channel your ancestors and receive guidance from the other side.

6. Coming out of the Trance State

After you've finished channeling your ancestors, it's very important that you carefully and slowly come out of the trance state. To do this, begin by focusing and taking a few deep breaths. Then, open your eyes and take a look around the room. Take a few moments to stretch and move your body before getting up and resuming your day. Remember that channeling can be a very powerful experience, so take some time to ground yourself afterward. By following these simple steps, you can ensure that you have a safe and successful experience channeling your ancestors.

7. Practice

If you're interested in spirit channeling, you may be wondering how to get started. After all, it's not something that you can just pick up overnight. However, the good news is that practice does make perfect. Many people are interested in channeling their ancestors but don't know how to go about it. The first step is to enter into a trance state. This can be done through meditation, prayer, or simply focusing your attention on your breath.

Once you have entered the trance state, relax and allow the energy of your ancestors to flow through you. You may feel them speaking to you or simply receive impressions and images. Trust whatever comes through, and do not try to force the experience. If you do feel called to speak aloud, do so respectfully and lovingly. Remember that your ancestors are here to help and guide you; they will do so in whatever way they feel is best.

Spirit Channeling Tips

If you've ever felt called to connect with the other side, you may wonder how to start channeling spirits. Here are some steps to help you:

1. Find a quiet place where you feel comfortable and relaxed. This will be your space for channeling, so make sure it's a place where you won't be interrupted.
2. Sit or recline in a comfortable position. You may want to close your eyes to help focus your attention inward.
3. Take several deep breaths and focus on letting go of any distractions or worries. Try to clear your mind and simply be present in the moment.
4. Once you feel centered and calm, focus your attention on your breath. Breathe deeply and slowly, and imagine each breath opening up your energy channels.
5. Visualize a white light emanating from your heart, filling your entire body with its peaceful, cleansing energy.
6. Now, invite the spirits you wish to communicate with to enter your light-filled space. Imagine them joining you in this safe and sacred space.
7. Ask the spirits any questions, and open yourself up to receive messages from them. You may hear them clearly in your mind, or they may come through as more subtle impressions or feelings. Trust whatever form the communication takes.
8. Thank the spirits for their time and guidance, and then visualize the white light again, this time expanding outward to engulf the space around you and drive away any negative energies that may have attached themselves to you during the channeling session.
9. When you're ready, slowly open your eyes and take a few minutes to journal about your experience. Write down anything that stands out to you, no matter how small it may seem. Review these tips regularly until they become second

nature! The more you practice, the easier it will be to channel spirits effectively—and safely!

Spirit channeling is a powerful way to connect with the other side and receive guidance from your ancestors. Mediumship and spirit channeling are different in that mediumship is passing on messages from the beyond, while spirit channeling is communicating directly with spirits. Shamanism, voodoo, and spiritualism are all different traditions that perceive and practice spirit channeling in different ways—but they all share the commonality of the trance state.

To channel spirits, you must first create a sacred space for yourself. This can be anywhere in your home where you feel comfortable and relaxed. Make sure to remove any distractions from this space, such as phones or television. You may also want to light some candles or incense to help set the mood. Once you're in your sacred space, take a few deep breaths and focus on your intention. Visualize your ancestors coming to you and ask them for guidance. Then, simply allow yourself to open up and receive whatever messages they have for you.

Remember, there's no right or wrong way to do this. Just go with the flow and trust that whatever comes through is meant for you. With a little practice, you'll be well on your way to channeling your ancestors!

Chapter 7: Channel Your Spirit Guides

As we journey through life, it can often feel like we are alone in the world. However, there is no need to feel like that, as we all have spirit guides who are there to help us. Spirit guides are powerful helpers who are always with us, even though we may not be aware of their presence. They can assist us in many ways, such as helping us with finding our purpose in life, providing comfort in times of difficulty, and guiding us when we need it most.

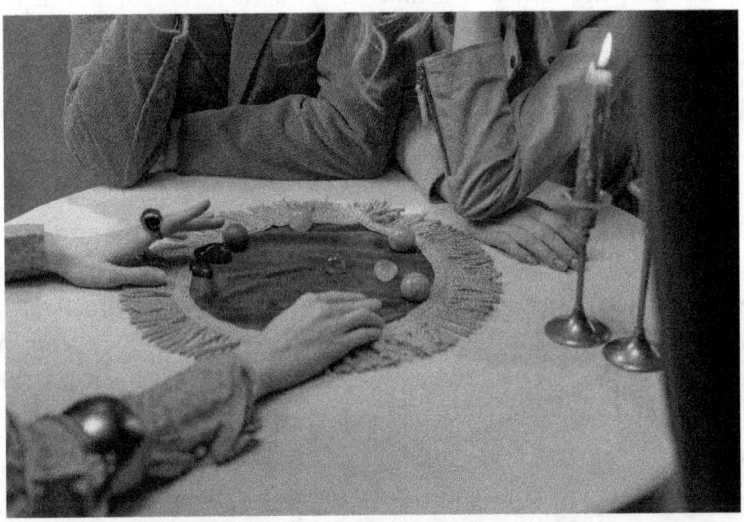

Many people believe in the existence of spirit guides.
https://www.pexels.com/photo/person-in-green-long-sleeve-shirt-sitting-on-brown-chair-7182627/

When we open ourselves up to the help of our spirit guides, we can live more fulfilling and joyful lives. This chapter will teach you about the different types of spirit guides that are available to help you on your journey. You'll also learn about some simple visualization exercises that can help you to connect with them. Finally, you'll be given tips on channeling your spirit guides so that you can receive their guidance more easily.

Spirit Guides

Many believe in spirit guides – unseen beings offering wisdom, guidance, and support. While some believe that we are each assigned a single spirit guide, others believe that we can have multiple guides – depending on our needs. Some say their guides come to them in dreams or meditation, while others claim to have never seen or heard their guides.

A spirit guide is an entity that is here to help us on our journey through life. They are often referred to as our guardian angels but can take many different forms. Spirit guides can be animals, plants, or even inanimate objects. They can also be deceased loved ones, such as a grandparent or close friend. It is believed that we each have at least one spirit guide, but we may have many more.

Whether or not you believe in the existence of spirit guides, there's no denying that they make for interesting stories. Guides are often said to be wise and all-knowing and are usually used as a force for good. Suppose you're ever feeling lost or confused. In that case, it might be worth considering the possibility that you have a spirit guide who is trying to help you find your way.

Types of Spirit Guides

There are many different types of spirit guides, each with a unique role to play in our lives. Some guides can help us to find our purpose, those who offer comfort and support, and those who give us practical advice. Whatever their form, spirit guides can offer us guidance, support, and protection when we need it most. Here are some of the most common types of spirit guides:

1. Angels

Angels are beings of light and love and are often called upon to provide guidance and support during difficult times. They can also help us connect with our higher selves and true purpose in life. While we all have guardian angels who watch over us, we can also choose to work with other angels who can offer specific types of support and guidance. If you feel called to work with an angel, there are many ways to go about it. You can meditate on their energy, ask for their help during prayer or visualization, or even keep a picture of them nearby as a reminder of their presence. However you choose to connect with them, know they are always here to support and guide you on your journey.

2. Spirit Animals

Many cultures believe that each person has a spirit animal, which is a reflection of their inner self. The idea of a spirit animal is thought to have originated with the shamans of ancient times, who would communicate with animals to gain wisdom and understanding. Many modern-day cultures have adopted this concept, which is now seen as a way to connect with nature and the animal kingdom. People often choose their spirit animal based on qualities they admire or identify with. For example, someone who is courageous might choose a lion as their spirit animal, while someone wise might choose an owl. By connecting with their spirit animal, people hope to gain some of the positive qualities that the animal possesses.

3. Plant Allies

In many cultures, plants are seen as powerful allies and teachers. For centuries, indigenous peoples have relied on plant medicine for physical and spiritual healing. Today, working with plant spirits is known as "plant ally work."

Plant ally work can take many forms. Some people work with plant spirits for guidance and wisdom, while others use plant medicine for healing. Some people even choose to live in close relationships with plants, spending time in nature and learning from the ones around them.

There are many ways to connect with plant spirits. One common practice is to spend time in nature and simply open yourself up to receiving guidance from the plants. You can also try asking specific questions and then listening for the answer in your heart. Many people find it helpful to keep a journal to record their experiences and insights.

If you're interested in working with plant spirits, many resources are available to help you get started. Books, websites, and even online courses can introduce you to the basics of plant ally work. You may also want to seek out a local teacher or shaman who can guide you on your journey. Remember that the most crucial thing is to follow your heart and trust your intuition.

4. Deceased Loved Ones

Many believe that we are all accompanied by spirit guides throughout our lives. These guides can take many different forms, but one of the most common is that of a deceased loved one. It is thought that our loved ones choose to stay with us after death to help us through difficult times and offer guidance when needed. Some people say that they have received guidance from a deceased loved one in dreams or visions, while others claim to have heard their voice during meditation or moments of clarity. While there is no scientific proof of the existence of spirit guides, the belief provides comfort and hope for many people. Whether or not you believe in spirit guides, it is clear that the idea of having a deceased loved one watch over you can be a source of great comfort.

5. Ascended Masters

The Ascended Masters are one of the most well-known types of spirit guides. These are beings who have reached a high level of spiritual development and now serve as mentors and teachers for those still on our spiritual journey. They can take on many different forms and often appear to us in our dreams or meditation. They are here to help us learn, grow, and develop our spiritual gifts. If you feel called to work with an Ascended Master, know that a powerful force is guiding you for good. Trust your intuition and follow your heart. You are being led in the right direction.

Visualization Exercises

If you're looking to connect with your spirit guide, one of the best things you can do is simply close your eyes and visualize. Picture your guide in whatever form they take – human, animal, or even a ball of light. See them standing or floating next to you, and imagine yourself reaching out to touch them. As you focus on this image, see if any feelings or impressions come to mind. Do they have a message for you? Are they trying to show you something?

Just allow whatever comes to your flow freely, and don't try to force anything. Remember, the goal is simply to relax and open yourself up to receiving guidance from your spirit guide. With a little practice, you should be able to connect with them anytime, anywhere. Here are different ways you can work with your spirit guide, depending on what form they take:

1. Connecting with Your Angels

Imagine yourself in a beautiful meadow surrounded by friendly animals. The sun is shining, and the breeze is gentle. You feel safe and loved. You see two angelic beings standing next to you as you look around. They radiate love and light and are here to protect and support you. Listen to what they have to say. What do they tell you about your life Purpose? What do they offer guidance about? Thank them for their help, and then let them go.

Return to the present moment, and take some time to journal about your experience. How did it feel to connect with your angels? What wisdom did they share with you? Allow this visualization exercise to deepen your understanding of your relationship with the divine realm.

2. Connecting with Your Spirit Animal

Close your eyes and take a few deep breaths. Imagine yourself in a field of tall grass. The sun is shining, and the breeze is blowing. You see a path in front of you, and you begin to walk along this path. As you do, you notice a beautiful creature standing in the distance. It is your spirit animal. As you approach, the animal comes to meet you. It looks into your eyes and nuzzles your hand. You feel a sense of peace and connection with this creature. You spend some time together, and then the animal runs off into the distance. As you watch it go, you feel refreshed and uplifted. This is your spirit animal, and it is always with you, guiding and supporting you on your journey through life.

3. Connecting with a Deceased Loved One

It can be difficult to cope with the loss of a loved one. Even if we know that they are no longer suffering, it can be hard to let go. One way to facilitate the grieving process is through visualization exercises. Connecting with a deceased loved one through visualization can create a sense of closure and peace.

To begin, find a comfortable place to sit or lie down. Close your eyes and take a few deep breaths. Once you are feeling relaxed, picture your loved one in your mind's eye. They may appear as they did in life or come to you in a different form. Allow yourself to spend some time simply enjoying their company. Then, ask them any of the questions you have been carrying around since their death. You may want to ask about their experience of dying, what they see now, or what message they would like to share with you. Listen carefully to their answers, and trust that whatever they tell you is meant for you and will help you to heal. Finally, say goodbye and allow them to go. Thank them for coming to visit.

When you are finished, take a few minutes to journal about your experience. What did you see? What did your loved one tell you? How do you feel now? Allow yourself to process whatever comes up for you, knowing that each time you connect with your loved one in this way, it will become easier and more natural.

4. Connecting with Ascended Masters

As you close your eyes and begin to relax, take a few deep breaths and allow your mind to wander. Picture yourself in a beautiful garden, surrounded by blue sky and white clouds. In the center of the garden is a large tree, and sitting at the base of the tree is an Ascended Master. This being of light is benevolent and wise, and they are here to help you on your journey.

As you approach, the Ascended Master smiles and opens their arms to you. You feel a sense of peace and love as you embrace them. Then, ask the Ascended Master any question that is on your mind. Listen carefully to their answer, and trust that they are guiding you in the right direction. Thank them for their time, and then slowly open your eyes and return to the present moment. Take a few deep breaths, and know you are always connected to the Ascended Masters.

5. Connecting with a Plant Ally

Plants are living beings and are here to help us in our journey through life. When we connect with them in a spirit of love and respect, they can teach us many things. To connect with a plant ally, find a comfortable place to sit or lie down. Close your eyes and take a few deep breaths. Picture yourself in a beautiful meadow surrounded by wildflowers. In the distance, you see a tree that is calling you.

As you approach, you notice the tree glowing with a soft light. You reach out and place your hand on the tree trunk, and you feel a deep connection with this being. Ask the tree any question on your mind, and then listen carefully to the answer. Thank the tree for its time, and then slowly open your eyes and return to the present moment. Take a few deep breaths, and know that you are always connected to the plant kingdom.

How to Channel Your Spirit Guides

We all have spirit guides – those unseen helpers who offer guidance and support on our life journey. Unfortunately, many of us are not attuned to their presence and their wisdom. If you're seeking to connect with your guides, you can do a few things to channel their energy.

1. Meditation

Channeling your spirit guides can provide you with invaluable insights and guidance. One of the best ways to connect with your guides is through meditation. Before you begin, find a comfortable place to sit or lie down. Close your eyes and take a few deep breaths. Once you're feeling relaxed, start to focus on your breath. Slowly exhale and, as you do, visualize a white light emanating from your heart. This light will help to ground and protect you as you open yourself up to the energies of the Universe.

Next, imagine a golden cord connecting your heart to the infinite source of love and light. Take a few deep breaths and allow yourself to be filled with this divine energy. When you're ready, begin asking your guides for guidance or clarity on a specific issue. Be open to receiving whatever messages come through, whether it's in the form of images, words, or feelings. After you've finished meditating, take a few minutes to journal about your experience. Don't worry if you didn't receive any clear messages at first. It can sometimes take a bit of practice to channel your guides. With time and patience, you'll be able to connect with them whenever you need their guidance.

2. Automatic Writing

Channeling your spirit guides can be a great way to receive guidance and clarity on your life path. Another approach to communicating with your guides is automatic writing. It is a form of channeling where you allow the thoughts and words of your spirit guides to flow through you and onto the page. To practice automatic writing, find a quiet place where you won't be interrupted. Sit down with a pen and paper, and take a few deep breaths to relax your mind and body. Then, simply allow your hand to move across the paper, writing whatever words or thoughts come naturally from your hand.. Trust that whatever you write comes from a place of love and guidance, and be open to receiving whatever messages your guides have for you.

3. Psychometry

Psychometry is a psychic ability that allows people to receive information about an object or person by touching it. It is believed that everyone can use psychometry, but some people are more attuned to it than others. To try it for yourself, all you need is an object that belongs to the person you want to connect with. Once you have the object, hold it in your hands and focus on it. As you do so, try to clear your mind and open yourself up to any impressions or messages that come through. You may experience visions, hear voices, or simply get a sense of the person's energy. There is no right or wrong way to do this, so go with whatever feels most natural to you. With a little practice, you should be able to use psychometry to connect with your spirit guides and receive the guidance you seek.

4. Divination

Divination is a great way to start if you're curious about connecting with your spirit guides. Divination is the practice of using tools like tarot cards, crystal balls, or runes to gain insight into the future or to receive guidance from one's spirit guides. While some people view divination as a way to predict the future, it can also be used as a tool for self-exploration and growth. If you're interested in trying divination, there are many different techniques to choose from. Some popular methods include tarot reading, rune casting, and scrying. When choosing a method, it's important to go with what feels right for you. Trust your intuition and let your spirit guides guide you to the divination method that is best for you.

5. Dreaming

Dreams are a way for our subconscious mind to communicate with us, and they can be powerful tools for self-discovery. To channel your spirit guides through dreaming, start by keeping a dream journal. Write down your dreams as soon as you wake up, including as many details as possible. Then, start to notice any patterns that emerge. Are there certain symbols or messages that keep appearing? These may be signs from your spirit guides. Pay attention to your feelings and intuition when interpreting your dreams, as this is how your guides will communicate with you. With a little practice, you'll be able to channel your spirit guides through dreaming and receive the guidance you need.

Spirit guides are powerful allies that can offer guidance and support on your spiritual journey. It can be a guardian angel, a plant ally, an animal guide, or any other type of divine being that you feel a connection. If you're interested in connecting with your spirit guides, you can use many different techniques. Some popular methods include trance channeling, automatic writing, psychometry, divination, and dreaming. Trust your intuition and let your spirit guides guide you to the method that is best for you. Keep an open mind and trust whatever messages you receive. With a little practice, you'll be able to connect with your spirit guides and receive the guidance you seek.

Chapter 8: Cleansing and Protecting Yourself

As a medium, it's crucial to keep yourself and your environment clean. Regular cleansing removes any negativity you may have picked up from spiritual work and protects you from unwanted attachments. There are lots of different ways to cleanse yourself and your home, so choose the method that feels right for you. You may want to burn sage or palo santo, use crystals or smudge sticks, or simply take a salt bath. Remember that cleansing is an ongoing process, so regularly cleanse yourself and your space.

It's crucial to cleanse yourself before and after each seance or reading.
https://www.pexels.com/photo/photo-of-sage-beside-rose-quartz-4040591/

This chapter will teach you the importance of cleansing, different methods, and how to perform various cleansing rituals. You'll also learn about banishing rituals, which remove negative energy, curses, or entities from your home. By the end of this chapter, you'll be equipped with the knowledge you need to keep yourself and your environment safe and clean.

Importance of Cleansing

Cleansing is an essential part of being a medium. As you open yourself up to the spiritual world, you become more susceptible to picking up negative energy. This can lead to problems like psychic attacks, possession, and even depression. Cleansing yourself and your environment regularly helps to protect you from these negative energies and attachments. Cleaning yourself before and after each seance or reading is also crucial, as this will help remove any unwanted energies you may have picked up during the session.

1. Helps to Remove Negativity

Cleansing removes any unwanted energies that may have gotten attached to you and promotes balance and harmony within your energy field. There are several different ways to cleanse yourself, but one of the most effective is using crystals. Crystals can help to absorb and release negative energies, and they can also help to promote a sense of calm and well-being. If you want to cleanse yourself regularly, then using crystals is worth considering.

2. Protects You from Psychic Attacks

There are a few different ways you can cleanse yourself. One is to use sage or Palo Santo wood. Simply hold the wood in your hand and smudge yourself with it, starting at your head and moving down to your feet. You can also cleanse yourself with crystals. Place a few stones on your body and allow their energy to flow through you. Another option is to take a salt bath. Add some Himalayan salt or Epsom salt to your bathwater and relax for 20 minutes. As you soak, visualize the water cleansing your aura and washing away any negativity. By cleansing yourself regularly, you'll stay protected from psychic attacks and maintain a healthy energy field.

3. Reduces the Risk of Attachment

Mediumship can be a rewarding and life-changing experience, but it also comes with some inherent risks. One of the most common risks is attachment – when the spirit of a deceased individual begins to attach itself to the medium. This can be harmful to both parties, as it can prevent the medium from moving on and living their life. Cleansing is one way to reduce the risk of attachment, as it helps clear away any residual energy clinging to the medium. There are many different ways to cleanse, but some common methods include sage smudging, crystal cleansing, and sacred baths. Taking time to cleanse after each mediumship session can help reduce the risk of attachment and keep yourself healthy and balanced.

4. Can Help You to Develop Your Skills

Cleansing can clear away any negative energy that might be clinging to you, and it can also help to raise your vibration. This, in turn, can make it easier for you to connect with spirit Guides and loved ones who have passed on. When you're free from negative energy, you'll be able to focus more clearly on your mediumship skills and develop them more quickly. The more you practice, the better you'll become at connecting with the other side.

5. Protects from Possession and Depression

One of the most vital things you can do as a medium is cleansing yourself regularly. Not only will this remove any negative energy that you may have picked up, but it will also protect you from possession and help you stay grounded and connected to your guides. Some of the best ways to cleanse yourself include sage smudging, crystal cleansing, and salt baths. By cleaning regularly, you can help keep yourself safe and healthy and develop your mediumship skills more quickly.

Methods of Cleansing

While every medium will have their preferred method of cleansing, there are a few that are more commonly used. Here are some of the most popular ones:

1. Smudging

Smudging is a ceremonial way of cleansing and purifying a space or person with the smoke of specific dried herbs. Some of the most popular herbs for smudging include sage, sweetgrass, and cedar. When smudging, it is crucial to set your intention. For example, you may want to cleanse your space of negative energy or invite in positive energy. Once your intention is set, light the herb and allow it to smolder. Wash the smoke around your body or space using your hand or a feather. Start at the feet and move up to the head. As you do this, visualize the smoke taking away any negative energy. Once you have cleansed yourself or your space, extinguish the herb and thank it for its service.

2. Visualization

One method that can be especially effective for cleansing is visualization. This involves picturing yourself surrounded by white light or any other type of light you feel drawn to. As you picture the light surrounding you, visualize it cleansing your aura and washing away any negativity. You may also want to visualize the light entering your body and filling you with positive energy.

To visualize, simply close your eyes and picture a white light surrounding your body. This light will help to cleanse your energy field and remove any negative or unwanted energies. Visualize the light moving up and down your body, starting at your feet and moving up to your head. Take a few deep breaths and allow yourself to relax into the visualization. Once you feel that you have been fully cleansed, you can open your eyes and resume your work.

3. Reiki

Reiki is a method of natural healing that can be used to cleanse and balance the body's energy systems. It is based on the belief that an invisible life force energy surrounds the bodies. When this energy is in balance, we are healthy and well. Reiki works by channeling this life force energy into the body through the hands of a trained practitioner. This breaks up any blockages or imbalances in the flow of energy, allowing the body to heal itself. Reiki is a gentle and effective way to cleanse the body and promote healing, and it can be used on both people and animals. If you are interested in trying Reiki, many qualified practitioners would be happy to help you experience its benefits.

4. Crystals

As a medium, it is crucial to keep your energy field clean and free of negative attachments. There are many ways to do this, but cleansing crystals is one of the most effective. They can help to remove negative energy from your auric field, as well as help protect you from further psychic attacks. When selecting crystals for cleansing, choose those that resonate with your energy field. Some of the most popular crystals for cleansing include amethyst, black tourmaline, and selenite. These stones can be used in various ways, such as being placed on your body during meditation or worn as jewelry. In whichever way you choose to use them, incorporating cleansing crystals into your mediumship practice can help ensure that you operate from a place of purity and light.

5. Sound Healing

Sound healing is a method of cleansing for mediums that uses sound waves to cleanse and balance the energy in your space. This type of cleansing is said to be especially effective for removing negative energy and promoting physical and emotional healing. Sound healing can be used in a variety of ways, such as through the use of singing bowls, chimes, or gongs. It can also be done simply by listening to calming music or sounds.

To use sound healing for cleansing, simply find a comfortable place to sit or lie down. Close your eyes and begin to focus on your breath. As you breathe in and out, allow the sound of the music or instruments to wash over you. Visualize the sound waves entering your body and cleansing your aura. Continue to breathe deeply and focus on the sound until you feel that you have been fully cleansed.

Cleansing Rituals

As a medium, it is vital to regularly cleanse your energy field to maintain your psychic ability. Negativity can build up over time, and it is essential to release this energy regularly. There are many different ways to cleanse your energy, and you can choose the method or methods that work best for you. Some people prefer to do a full-body cleansing ritual daily, while others may only do it once a week or so. Listen to your body and intuition to determine what is best for you. Nevertheless, here are a few popular cleansing rituals that you may want to try:

1. Full Moon Cleanse

Full moon cleanses are a great way to release old energy and make space for new beginnings. A full moon cleansing ritual can be done alone or with a group of other mediums. To begin, sit or stand in a circle. If you are using candles, place them in the center of the circle. Take a few deep breaths and focus on your intention for the cleansing. Then, each person in the circle should say aloud one thing that they would like to release. This can be anything that is no longer serving you, such as a negative emotion or belief.

Once everyone has spoken, take a few minutes to meditate on what you are letting go of. When you are ready, start the cleansing by visualizing white light entering your body and pushing out any negativity. You can also use sage or palo santo to cleanse your energy field. Continue until you feel cleansed and balanced.

2. New Moon Cleanse

A new moon cleansing is similar to a full moon cleansing. Still, it focuses on setting future intentions rather than releasing old energy. This can be done in several ways, but some basic steps include: clearing your home of negative energy, setting intentions for the month ahead, and cleansing your body and mind. To clear your home, you can smudge with sage or palo santo, use an energy spray, or simply open all the doors and windows to let fresh air in.

Once your home is cleared, you can set your intentions by writing them down on a piece of paper or creating a vision board. Finally, cleanse your body and mind by taking a salt bath, drinking plenty of water, and meditating. Performing this ritual at the beginning of each month will help keep your energy clean and aligned with your highest self.

3. Solar Eclipse Cleanse

A solar eclipse is an ideal time to cleanse your energy field, as the increased energies can help release any heaviness or negativity you may be carrying. There are many different ways to perform a solar eclipse cleanse. One simple method is to take a saltwater bath using either Epsom salts or sea salt. You can also add a few drops of lavender oil to help promote relaxation and peace.

As you take your bath, imagine the water washing away any unwanted energies, leaving you feeling refreshed and rejuvenated. When you're done, make sure to drink plenty of water to help flush any toxins from your system. Regular cleansing rituals like this can help ensure that your energy field is clear and free-flowing.

4. Lunar Eclipse Cleanse

A lunar eclipse is another powerful time to cleanse your energy field. This can be done similarly to a solar eclipse cleansing – but with a few tweaks to suit the moon's energies. For example, you may want to add some lunar-associated herbs to your baths, such as jasmine or chamomile. You can also add a few drops of moonstone oil to your bathwater. This stone is particularly helpful in releasing emotions and past traumas. As with a solar eclipse, imagine the water washing away any negative energy, leaving you feeling lighter and brighter. When you've finished, make sure you drink plenty of water to help flush any toxins from your system.

5. Equinox Cleanse

As the seasons change, it can be a good time to cleanse your body, mind, and spirit. One way to do this is through a cleansing ritual. There are many different types of cleansing rituals, but one that is particularly well-suited for mediums is an Equinox Cleanse. This type of cleansing helps to realign your energy with the changing energies of the Earth. To perform this, you'll need a bowl of salt water, a white candle, and a piece of quartz crystal.

Begin by lighting the candle and placing it in front of you. Then, hold the quartz crystal in your left hand and dip it into the salt water. As you do this, visualize your life's negativity being washed away. Next, take a deep breath and release it slowly. Repeat this process three times. Finally, blow out the candle and allow the quartz crystal to air dry. As you perform this cleansing ritual, you should feel your energy shifting and aligning with the Earth's natural rhythms.

6. Solstice Cleanse

December is a month full of holidays and celebrations. For many people, it is a time to reflect on the past year and set their intention for the year to come. It is also a time when the veil between the spiritual and physical worlds is at its thinnest. As a result, December is an ideal time for mediums to perform a cleansing ritual. The solstice cleanse is a simple but powerful ritual that can help to clear away any unwanted energy and prepare you for the year ahead.

To begin, light a white candle and say: "I release all that no longer serves me. I welcome only that which is for my highest good." Then, take a few deep breaths and imagine yourself surrounded by white light. Visualize the light cleansing your aura of any negative energy. Next, hold each of your crystals in the candle flame for a few seconds, saying: "I cleanse you of all negativity." Finally, bury your crystals in the earth overnight, releasing any remaining unwanted energy. By performing this cleansing ritual, you'll help to create a space for positive energy to flow into your life.

Banishment Rituals

Banishment rituals are a necessary part of being a medium. As a medium, you are constantly surrounded by good and bad spirits. It is essential to keep the bad spirits away so they do not influence your work or harm those around you. There are many different banishment rituals that you can use, but the most crucial thing is that you are comfortable with the ritual and that it works for you. Some people prefer to use salt or holy water, while others use more elaborate rituals involving candles and incantations. Ultimately, the choice is up to you. Just remember that banishing rituals are vital to being a responsible medium.

1. Banishing Ritual for Negative Energy

There are certain banishing rituals that you can do to cleanse your space and get rid of any unwanted energy. One simple but effective method is to smudge your home with sage. This will help to clear the air and create a more positive vibration. You can also try using crystals such as selenite or black tourmaline to absorb negative energy. If you find yourself regularly surrounded by negative influences, it may be time to take a break from mediumship and focus on raising your vibration. By doing this, you'll be better equipped to handle any negativity that comes your way.

2. Banishing Ritual for a Curse or Hex

Suppose you suspect that you or someone you know has been cursed or hexed by a malicious spirit. In that case, you can take steps to banish the negative energy and protect yourself from further harm. First, understand that curses and hexes are a very real part of the spiritual world and should not be taken lightly. If you think you may have been cursed, you should first seek help from a medium or psychic who can assess the situation and identify the source of the curse.

Once the source has been identified, the medium will then work with you to perform a banishing ritual. This usually involves cleansing the area with sage smoke or holy water and then using powerful visualization techniques to force the negative energy out. With the help of a skilled medium, banishing curses and hexes is relatively straightforward – but it's always best to be cautious and take precautions to protect yourself from these dark forces.

3. Banishing Ritual for Ghosts, Spirits, and Entities

Suppose you are regularly dealing with ghosts, spirits, or entities. In that case, it is critical to have a reliable banishing ritual that you can use to send them away. This ritual should be performed whenever you feel like you are being followed or watched by an unwanted presence. To begin, light a white candle and say: "I banish you from this space. You are not welcome here." Then, use your fingers to trace a circle around the candle three times clockwise. As you do this, visualize a protective barrier forming around you. Finally, blow out the candle and say: "I release you from this space. You are free to go." This banishing ritual will clear your space and protect you from any unwanted entities.

Cleansing and banishing rituals are a necessary part of being a medium. These rituals will also create a more positive vibration in your space, benefiting you and those around you. This chapter provided an overview of some basic cleansing and banishing rituals that you can use to protect yourself. Remember, the most crucial thing is to find a method that works for you and that you feel comfortable with. With the help of these cleansing and banishing rituals, you can keep yourself safe and protected from any negative influences.

Chapter 9: The Power of Scrying

Scrying is an ancient practice that has been used for centuries to gain insight and knowledge. It has been used for everything from divination and fortune-telling to communicating with spirits and gaining spiritual guidance. While the exact origins of scrying are unknown, it is thought to date back to at least the early Egyptians, who used polished obsidian mirrors for scrying.

Scrying is an ancient practice that has been used for centuries to gain insight and knowledge.
https://www.pexels.com/photo/crop-soothsayer-predicting-fate-with-magic-ball-at-home-4790577/

Today, many people worldwide still practice scrying, who believe in its power to offer insights and knowledge that can be difficult to obtain through other means. Whether looking for answers to life's big questions or simply seeking guidance from your higher self, scrying may be worth a try. This chapter will teach you everything you need to know about scrying, from the different types to how to interpret your visions.

Scrying Defined

Scrying is a practice that has been used for centuries for divination and fortune-telling. The word "scrying" comes from the Old English word "descry," which means "to reveal." Scrying is typically done by gazing into a crystal ball, a mirror, a bowl of water, or any other reflective surface. As you gaze at the surface, you may see images appear before your eyes. These images can be interpreted in many ways, depending on the person doing the scrying.

Some people believe that images are premonitions of future events, while others believe that they are symbols that must be interpreted. Scrying is a deeply personal practice, and there is no right or wrong way to do it. Whether you use a traditional method like crystal ball gazing or something more unique like tea leaf reading, the important thing is to relax and let your mind be open to whatever messages may come through.

There are many different ways to scry, and each person may have their preferences. Some common methods include using a crystal ball, a pool of water, a mirror, or a flame. When scrying, it is important to enter into a relaxed state of mind to allow messages from the other side to come through. Once you have entered into a meditative state, you can begin to focus on your question or intent. The answer may come in the form of symbols, images, or words. Scrying can be an effective way to receive guidance from the other side and connect with your intuition. With practice, anyone can learn how to scry.

Crystal Ball Scrying

Scrying is an ancient art that involves gazing into a reflective surface to induce a trance-like state. Crystal balls have been used for scrying since at least the 16th century and are still popular among modern-day practitioners. There are a few different ways to use a crystal ball for scrying. One method is simply gazing into the ball and allowing your mind to wander. Another way is to ask a question and then wait for an image or symbol to appear in the ball. Some people also like to light candles or incense and create a relaxing atmosphere before scrying. Whatever method you choose, remember that the most important thing is to relax and let your intuition guide you.

Pros and Cons

Scrying is one of the oldest and most popular forms of divination, with roots in ancient cultures such as Egypt, Greece, and China. The method can be used for navigation purposes, finding lost objects, or even communicating with spirits. While many people believe that scrying is a powerful tool for gaining insight into the future, there are also some drawbacks to this form of divination. One downside is that it can be difficult to interpret the images that are seen in the crystal ball. This means that scrying can sometimes be more frustrating than helpful. Additionally, because scrying requires a great deal of concentration, it can be taxing on both the body and mind. For these reasons, weighing the pros and cons of scrying is important before deciding whether to try it.

Step-By-Step Instructions

If you've never tried scrying before, it can seem like a daunting task. However, with a little practice, anyone can learn.

1. Find a quiet, comfortable place where you won't be interrupted. Make sure the area is well-lit so you can see the crystal ball.
2. Sit in a comfortable position and hold the crystal ball in your hands. Close your eyes and take a few deep breaths.
3. When ready, open your eyes and gaze into the crystal ball. Allow your mind to wander and see what images appear.
4. If you have a question you would like answered, focus on that question as you gaze into the ball.
5. Once you're finished scrying, reflect on what you saw for a few moments. Write down any impressions or images you saw in a journal for future reference.

Fire Scrying

Fire Scrying is a technique that has been used for centuries as a way of divination and fortune-telling. Fire scrying uses fire as a focal point. The act of scrying involves staring into a fire to induce a trance-like state, during which visions and messages may be received. It can be an effective way to receive guidance from your higher self or spirit guides. It is a simple yet powerful method for tapping into your intuition and accessing hidden knowledge. Give it a try the next time you need some clarity or guidance.

Pros and Cons

Many people find fire scrying to be an effective way of gaining clarity and insights into their lives. Still, there are also some potential drawbacks to this practice. One downside of fire scrying is that it can be very hard on the eyes, and it is crucial to take breaks frequently to avoid eye strain. Additionally, some people find the flickering flames to be distracting or even unsettling. Finally, because fire scrying requires such intense focus, it is important to be in a quiet and safe place where you will not be interrupted. Despite these potential drawbacks, this type can be a powerful tool for those who know how to use it effectively.

Step-By-Step Instructions

If you've never tried fire scrying, here are some simple instructions to get you started.

1. Find a quiet, safe place where you can build a small fire. You'll also need a metal bowl or cauldron to place the fire in.
2. Once you have everything you need, build a small fire in the bowl or cauldron. Allow the flames to burn for a few minutes until they become steady.
3. Sit in front of the fire and gaze into the flames. Relax your mind and body, and let your thoughts flow freely.
4. After a few minutes, you may begin to see images or receive messages in the form of mental impressions. Write down any insights that you receive in a journal for future reference.

Water Scrying

Water scrying is an ancient practice. Also known as crystal gazing, water scrying involves staring into a bowl of water to reveal hidden messages or visions. While the practice may sound simple, it requires focus and concentration to work. Many people believe that water scrying is a powerful tool for divination, and it has been used for centuries to help people make important decisions. If you're interested in trying water scrying, all you need is a bowl of clean water and a quiet place to focus. You may not see anything right away, but with patience and practice, you may be surprised by what you can see.

Pros and Cons

Water scrying is a form of divination that involves gazing into a bowl of water to gain insight into the future. Some people believe that water scrying is more accurate than other forms of divination because water is a natural element that is connected to all life. Others argue that water scrying is no more accurate than any other form of fortune-telling. While no scientific evidence supports either claim, water scrying can be a fun and interesting way to gain insights into the future.

Water scrying can be an enjoyable way to pass the time and gain some insight into the future. However, remember that it should not be taken too seriously. Like all forms of fortune-telling, it should be considered entertainment rather than a source of true information about the future.

Step-By-Step Instructions

Several different techniques can be used for water scrying. If you're interested in trying water scrying, you need a bowl of clean water and a quiet place to focus.

1. Fill a bowl with clean water and set it in front of you. You may want to add a drop of food coloring to the water to make it easier to see.
2. Sit in front of the bowl and stare into the water. Relax your mind and body, and let your thoughts flow freely.
3. After a few minutes, you may begin to see images or receive messages in the form of mental impressions. Write down any insights that you receive in a journal for future reference.

Mirror Scrying

Mirror scrying is a type of divination that involves gazing into a reflective surface to gain information about the future. Although any type of mirror can be used for scrying, many people prefer to use black mirrors, as they believe they can better capture and reflect energy. When practicing, you may see images appear on the mirror's surface. These images can symbolize anything from future events to messages from your subconscious mind. With practice, you'll learn to interpret these images and use them to gain insights into your life.

Pros and Cons

While there are many potential benefits to this practice, there are also some drawbacks that should be considered. One of the main advantages of mirror scrying is that it can be done with very little equipment. All you need is a mirror and a quiet place to focus your attention. This makes it an ideal divination method for people who are just starting or who don't have access to more specialized tools. Additionally, it can be used for various purposes, from gaining self-knowledge to peering into other people's lives. However, there are also some disadvantages to consider.

One potential downside is that staring into a mirror for extended periods can be taxing on the eyes. It's important to take breaks and rest your eyes if you start to feel discomfort. Additionally, some people find that they become too focused on their reflection during mirror scrying sessions, which can prevent them from seeing the greater picture. If you find yourself getting too caught up in your image, it might be helpful to try using a black or dark-colored cloth to cover the mirror until you're ready to end your session.

Overall, mirror scrying is a versatile and effective form of divination that can yield valuable insights. However, as with any type of divination, it's important to approach it with caution and an open mind.

Step-By-Step Instructions

If you're interested in trying mirror scrying for yourself, all you need is a mirror and a quiet place to focus. To get started, follow these simple steps:

1. Find a mirror that's large enough for you to comfortably gaze into. A black mirror is often used for this purpose, but any type of mirror will work.
2. Place the mirror in front of you and sit down. Relax your mind and body, and let your thoughts flow freely.
3. After a few minutes, you may see images appear on the mirror's surface. These images can symbolize anything from future events to messages from your subconscious mind. Write down any insights you receive in a journal for future reference.

Ink Scrying

Ink scrying is a form of divination that involves looking at patterns in ink, coffee, or tea stains. As you look at the ink, you may start to see shapes and patterns forming. These shapes can be interpreted in several ways, depending on their appearance and placement on the paper. For example, a shape that resembles a heart may symbolize love, while a circle might represent unity or completeness. By interpreting the shapes you see, you can gain insight into your past, present, and future. Ink scrying is a simple but effective way to connect with your subconscious mind and uncover hidden truths.

Pros and Cons

Ink scrying is a relatively simple and inexpensive form of divination. All you need is a piece of paper, ink, coffee, or tea. Additionally, this method can be used for various purposes, from gaining self-knowledge to predicting the future. However, some drawbacks should be considered. One potential downside is that it can be difficult to interpret the shapes you see. If you're not experienced with this method, it's easy to mistake one shape for another.

Additionally, some people find that they become too focused on the patterns they see, which can prevent them from seeing the greater picture. If you find yourself getting too caught up in ink, it might be helpful to take a break and return to it later. Overall, ink scrying is a simple but powerful form of divination that can yield valuable insights. However, as with any type of divination, it's important to approach it with caution and an open mind.

Step-By-Step Instructions

If you're interested in trying ink scrying, all you need is a piece of paper, some ink, coffee, or tea. To get started, follow these simple steps:

1. Find a quiet place to work where you won't be disturbed.
2. Pour some ink, coffee, or tea onto a plate or shallow dish.
3. Dip your finger in the liquid and use it to draw shapes or patterns on a piece of paper.
4. As you look at the shapes you've created, allow your mind to wander and see what images or messages come to you.
5. Write down any insights you receive in a journal for future reference.

Smoke Scrying

Smoke scrying is a type of divination that involves observing the patterns formed by smoke. It can be done with any type of smoke, but incense is most commonly used. You may see images, symbols, or messages in the smoke. Allow whatever comes to you to be without judgment or analysis. Smoke scrying is a simple yet powerful way to connect with your intuition and receive guidance from the spirit world.

Pros and Cons

Many cultures have their methods of smoke scrying, and the practice has been used for centuries to help people make important decisions. There are pros and cons to smoke scrying, and it's crucial to weigh them before deciding whether this form of divination is right for you.

One of the biggest advantages of smoke scrying is that it can be done almost anywhere. All you need is a fire and some form of smoking material (such as herbs). This makes it a very convenient form of divination for people always on the go. Additionally, it can be a very personal experience. Since you interpret the smoke yourself, there is no need to rely on anyone else's opinion or interpretation. However, there are also some disadvantages.

One downside is that it can be difficult to correctly interpret the smoke. This form of divination requires a lot of practice and experience to become accurate. Additionally, because interpreting the smoke is such a personal experience, it's easy to let your biases influence your readings. Overall, smoke scrying is a unique and interesting form of divination with both pros and cons. Keep these in mind before deciding whether or not it's right for you.

Step-By-Step Instructions

If you're interested in trying smoke scrying, all you need is a fire and some form of smoking material (such as incense or herbs). To get started, follow these simple steps:

1. Find a quiet place to work where you won't be disturbed.
2. Light a fire in a safe place.
3. Add your smoking material to the fire.
4. Observe the patterns formed by the smoke.
5. Allow your mind to wander and see what images or messages come to you.
6. Write down any insights that you receive in a journal for future reference.

Overall, scrying is a powerful tool that can be used for divination and self-discovery. There are many different methods, each with its advantages and disadvantages. This chapter provides a brief overview of some of the most popular ones. Experiment with different techniques and find the one that works best for you. Remember to approach scrying with an open mind and let the information that comes to you flow in without judgment or analysis. With practice, you'll be able to use scrying to gain valuable insights into yourself and your life.

Chapter 10: Advanced Spirit World Communication Methods

Communicating with the spirit world can be a very rewarding experience. It can provide you with closure, answers to burning questions, or simply give you a sense of connection to something greater than yourself. In this chapter, we will explore some of the more advanced methods of spirit-world communication. These methods include using a pendulum, an Ouija board, tarot cards, and automatic writing. By the end of this chapter, you should understand how to use each of these methods and the pros and cons associated with each one.

Communicating with the spirit world can provide you with closure, answers to burning questions, or simply give you a sense of connection to something greater than yourself.
https://www.pexels.com/photo/hands-holding-the-crystal-ball-on-the-wooden-table-6806746/

Using a Pendulum for Spirit Communication

A pendulum is a weight, typically made of crystal, hung from a string or chain. Using one for spirit communication is a practice that dates back centuries. The pendulum is thought to be able to tap into the subconscious mind and connect with the spiritual realm. Pendulums are often used for divination and psychic readings. Many people believe that a pendulum can be used to communicate with the dead.

1. How to Use a Pendulum

There are a few different ways to use a pendulum for spirit communication. One way is to ask yes or no questions. The pendulum will swing in a certain direction to indicate the answer. Another way is to hold the pendulum over a sheet of paper with different symbols or words. The pendulum will swing toward the symbol or the word it is connected to.

If you are new to using a pendulum, it is best to start with simple questions. You may also want to have someone else hold the pendulum while you ask the questions. This will help eliminate any bias on your part. Once you get comfortable with using the pendulum, you can experiment with more complex questions. Remember, there are no wrong answers when communing with the spirits. Enjoy the process and see what wisdom they have to share with you!

2. Pros and Cons of Using a Pendulum

There are both pros and cons to using a pendulum for spirit communication. One pro is that it can be used by anyone, regardless of experience level. Another is that it does not require any special equipment or tools. All you need is a pendulum and something to write with. Pendulum use is not without its detractors. Some people believe that the pendulum can be influenced by the user's thoughts and feelings, making it unreliable as a method of communication. Others believe that the pendulum can be used to communicate with non-human entities, like demons and other dark forces. Despite these concerns, many people find the pendulum to be a useful tool for spirit communication and continue to use it.

3. Tips for Using a Pendulum

If you decide to use a pendulum for spirit communication, you should keep a few things in mind.

- Be in a relaxed state of mind. This will help you clear your mind and allow the pendulum to swing freely.
- Hold the pendulum over your dominant hand. This hand should be resting palm up on a flat surface.
- Ask your question out loud. This will help focus your thoughts and allow the pendulum to find the answer more easily.
- Be patient. The pendulum may not swing immediately. Give it a few moments to find the answer.
- Be open to whatever answer the pendulum gives. Remember, there are no wrong answers when communing with the dead.

Using a Ouija Board for Spirit Communication

A Ouija board is a board that is marked with the letters of the alphabet, numbers 0-9, and the words "yes," "no," and "hello." The board is used in conjunction with a planchette, a small heart-shaped piece of wood or plastic used to point to the different letters and symbols on the board. Many people believe that the Ouija board can be used to communicate with the dead.

1. How to Use a Ouija Board

Using a Ouija board is relatively simple. First, you need to gather a group of people together. Two is the minimum, but more can be used if desired. Next, you'll need to sit around the board and place your fingers on the planchette. Once everyone is ready, one person will ask a question out loud. The planchette will then begin to move around the board, spelling out the answer to the question.

2. Pros and Cons of Using a Ouija Board

Like any method of spirit communication, there are both pros and cons to using a Ouija board. One pro is that it can be a fun activity to do with friends or family. It can also connect with loved ones who have passed on. Another pro is that it is relatively easy to use and does not require special skills or knowledge.

There are also some cons. One is that it can be dangerous if not used correctly. There have been reports of people becoming possessed after using a Ouija board, so it is crucial to use caution. Another con is that the answers you receive may not always be accurate. This is because the planchette can be influenced by outside forces, such as wind or drafts.

3. Tips for Using a Ouija Board

If you decide to use a Ouija board, you should keep a few things in mind.

- Be respectful of the dead. This means not asking questions that could upset them or cause them to want to harm you.
- Be aware of your surroundings. Make sure that no drafts or wind could potentially move the planchette.
- Do not use the board alone. Always have at least one other person with you.
- Do not take the answers you receive at face value. Remember that they may not be accurate.

Using Tarot Cards for Spirit Communication

Tarot cards are cards used for divination. The deck is made up of 78 cards, which are divided into two groups: the Major Arcana and the Minor Arcana. The Major Arcana consists of 22 cards representing major life events or transitions. The Minor Arcana consists of 56 cards representing day-to-day challenges and experiences.

1. How to Use Tarot Cards for Spirit Communication

Tarot cards have been used for centuries as a tool for divination, but they can also be used for spirit communication. To use tarot cards for spirit communication, start by meditating and then asking your question out loud. Then, shuffle the deck and lay out the cards in a spread. Once the cards are laid out, focus on each one individually and ask your question again. As you do this, pay attention to any thoughts, feelings, or images that come to mind. These may be messages from your spirit guide or other spirits. If you're unsure what a message means, try looking up the card's symbolism in a book or online. With a little practice, you'll be able to use tarot cards for spirit communication.

2. Pros and Cons of Using Tarot Cards

Many people believe that tarot cards can be used as a tool for spirit communication. There are several different ways to use the cards for this purpose. While some people find tarot card readings to be accurate and helpful, others are skeptical of their ability to connect with spirits. Here are some pros and cons of using tarot cards for spirit communication:

Pros:
- Tarot card readings can be very accurate. Experienced readers can often interpret the messages of the cards very clearly.
- Readings can provide guidance and insight into important decisions. By connecting with spirits, tarot readers can receive guidance that may not be available through other means.
- These readings can be fun. Even if you don't believe in their ability to connect with spirits, tarot readings can be an enjoyable way to pass the time.

Cons:
- Some people believe that tarot card readings are inaccurate and misleading. There is no guarantee that the messages you receive from a tarot reading will be accurate or helpful.
- They can be expensive. If you hire a professional reader, you may have to pay quite a bit of money for their services.
- The readings can be intimidating. If you are unfamiliar with the process, it can be hard to know what to expect going into one.

3. Tips for Using Tarot Cards

If you decide to use tarot cards for spirit communication, you should keep a few things in mind.

- Make sure you are working with a reputable reader. There are many charlatans out there who will try to take advantage of people.
- Be clear about what you want to achieve from the reading. Before you begin, take some time to think about what you hope to gain from the experience. This will help you focus your questions and get the most out of the reading.
- Be open to the messages you receive. Don't try to force a particular outcome from the reading. Instead, let the messages come to you and trust that they are guidance from your spirit guide or other spirits.

Automatic Writing

Automatic writing is a spiritual practice that can be used to communicate with the other side. It is a form of channeling in which the writer surrenders their hand to a higher power and allows that higher power to write *through them*. This process can be done with a pen and paper or even with your finger if you are using a tablet or smartphone. The vital thing is to clear your mind and allow the words to flow. There is no need to worry about spelling or grammar, as the message will come through regardless. You may find that the words come slowly at first, but with practice, you'll be able to receive clear messages from your guides and loved ones who have passed on.

1. How to Perform Automatic Writing

Automatic writing is a simple process that anyone can do. It can be a powerful way to receive messages from the other side. To begin, find a quiet place where you will not be interrupted. Sit down with a pen and paper, and relax your mind. Once you feel calm, allow your hand to move freely across the page. As you write, trust that the words you receive are from the spirit world. The messages may not make sense at first, but if you keep writing, they will begin to form cohesive thoughts. If you keep an open mind, automatic writing can be a powerful tool for spirit communication.

2. Pros and Cons of Automatic Writing

There are many benefits to Automatic Writing. For one, it is a great way to receive messages from deceased loved ones. It can also be used to communicate with guides and angels. If you are looking for guidance on a particular issue, automatic writing can help you receive clarity.

There are also some drawbacks to Automatic Writing. It can be quite upsetting if you are not mentally or emotionally prepared to receive messages from the other side. Also, if you are not used to channeling energy, it can be easy to become fatigued. Setting aside time for relaxation before and after your session is crucial. Overall, this is a powerful tool that can be used for good or ill, depending on the user's intention. Use it wisely, and it will serve you well.

3. Tips for Automatic Writing

Here are a few tips to help you get the most out of your automatic writing experiences:

- Relax and clear your mind before beginning. The more relaxed you are, the easier it will be to receive messages.
- Set an intention for your session. What do you hope to achieve? Keep this in mind as you write.

- Be patient. The messages may not come immediately, but if you keep writing, they will come through.
- Be open to whatever comes through. You may not always understand the message, but trust that it is coming from a higher power.
- Take breaks as needed. If you feel tired or frustrated, take a break and return later.
- Keep a journal of your experiences. This will be a valuable resource to look back on later.

These are just a few of the many ways you can communicate with the other side. Experiment and find the method that works best for you. Always approach these experiences with an open mind and heart – and trust that the messages you receive are for your highest good. This chapter has provided some tips and background information on various mediumship methods. From here on, it is up to you to explore and find the ones that work best for you. So go forth and communicate with the other side!

Conclusion

Now that you have read all the information on mediumship, it's time to put it all together and start practicing! Remember, the most crucial thing is to relax and open yourself up to the experience. You'll be amazed at what you can do with a little practice!

This easy-to-follow guide has given you all the tools you need to develop your mediumship skills. It started with an introduction to the basics of mediumship and its workings. You learned about the different types of mediumship, as well as the astral body and the spirit world. You also learned some important techniques for grounding and preparing yourself before readings, as well as how to recognize energy.

After that, you dove right in, learning how to develop your clairvoyance skill. You also discovered spirit channeling and how to channel your spirit guides. Finally, you learned about advanced spirit world communication methods, like scrying, cleansing, and protecting yourself. The key to success is to relax and have fun with it!

If you want to try channeling your guides, start by doing some basic research. You can find plenty of resources online or at your local library. Once you understand the basics well, find a quiet place to relax and focus your thoughts. You may want to light a candle or burn some incense to help you relax and to create a sacred space. Then, simply ask your guides to come forward and communicate with you. You may want to ask specific questions or simply allow them to speak through you. Trust your intuition and go with whatever feels right.

Scrying is another great way to communicate with the spirit world. You can use a crystal ball, a bowl of water, a mirror, or any other shiny surface. Simply gaze into the surface and allow your mind to relax. You may see images or receive messages from your guides. Don't worry if you don't see or hear anything right away. It takes practice to develop your mediumistic abilities. Just keep trying, and eventually, you'll be amazed at what you can do.

While mediumship is a great way to connect with the spirit world, protecting yourself from negative energy is crucial. There are a few simple things you can do to protect yourself. First, always cleanse yourself and your space before you begin a session. You can use sage, salt water, or any other method you feel comfortable with. Second, always set your intention before you begin. Make sure that you are only working with positive, benevolent spirits. Finally, trust your intuition. If something doesn't feel right, just stop and walk away.

Mediumship is a great way to connect with the spirit world and receive guidance from your loved ones. You'll be amazed at what you can do with a little practice! Just remember to relax, go with your intuition, and have fun with it.

Part 2: Spirit Communication

Connecting with Spirit Guides, Ancestors, Archangels, and Angels, along with Developing Your Psychic Mediumship Abilities Such as Channeling and Clairvoyance

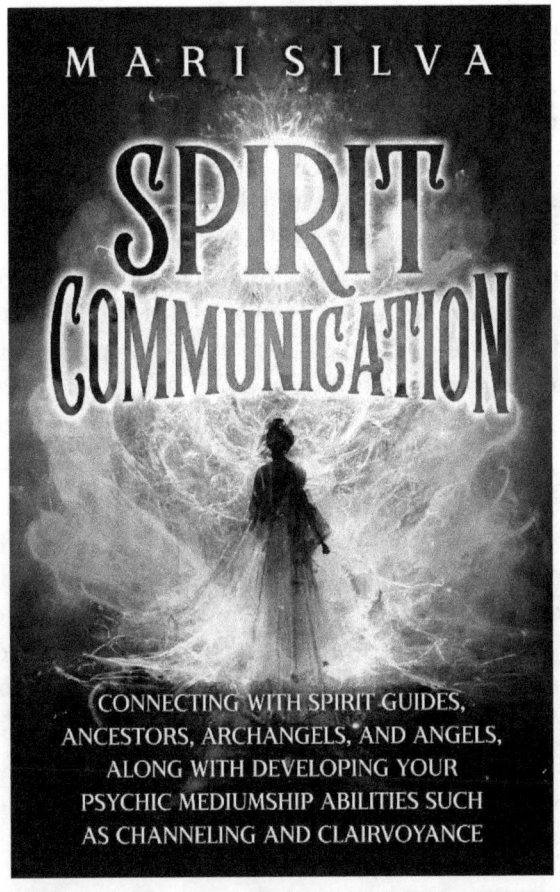

Introduction

So you want to connect with the beings beyond this world. You want to know how to receive knowledge from them so you can live a better life, figure out the things that leave you confused, and learn about your true purpose in life. You'd like to know that no matter where you are, you're never alone and can always reach out to get help from the unseen world. This is the best book to help you with those goals.

You may have decided that you'd like to reach out to the spirit of someone near and dear to you who has passed on. Maybe you just feel a presence around you, and you've decided that you'd like to connect with it and see what it's about. No matter your reason for connecting with spirits, you'll find this book full of excellent material to help you make it possible. As you dive into the contents of this book, don't be surprised if you begin to pick up on spiritual energies. Also, expect the unexpected in a good way.

This book will give you all the information you need in clear English. Every concept is explained clearly, and you'll have practical, down-to-earth, straightforward, and easy-to-read knowledge that you can act on. You're going to find exercises and methods you can use to get in touch with the spirits who are all around you. You'll also learn how to stay safe as you reach out to the other side while discovering that *there is nothing for you to be afraid of.*

The best thing about this book is that you will find the information provided is not the average stuff you get from page one of a Google search. You'll dive deep into the world of spirits and discover how reaching out to them will give you a richer, more rewarding life. It doesn't matter what religious beliefs you hold or if you're not into religion *at all*. You'll find that spirits do not discriminate against others as humans do. The information in the pages of this book is so good that you'll find you don't have to be a monk or a priest to be able to sense and connect with the spirits that hover around all day, every day. The information works because it's not about external, performative religion but about spirituality, which is the realization that there's much more to life than that which can be observed with our physical senses.

Whether you desire to gain valuable information or to experience spiritual growth, you'll find that there is no better way than to reach out to those who know far more than we could ever hope to - the spirits around us, all day, every day. You must understand that you must keep an open mind and temporarily suspend your disbelief. You don't have to let others know that this is what you're doing. As you use the information from this book, keeping an open mind will bring you phenomenal results. Let's get started if you're ready to explore the minds of those beyond this world.

Chapter 1: Can We Really Communicate with the Spirits?

Since the dawn of time, people have tried to reach out to the dead and other entities beyond this realm. Though every human body will eventually die, the spirit that powers it will continue to live on, and they have interests in the life they lived when they were human. Most people are aware of this on some level, and some are more than simply aware. These people go on to make attempts to connect with the spirits which have transitioned from this life, hoping to remain in touch with them or gain information from them.

Spirits are a consciousness that has transitioned from this world but is still alive.
https://www.pexels.com/photo/mediums-sitting-in-circle-holding-hands-7267688/

Think about the number of times you've thought about calling someone, only to do so and find out they're going through something at that moment. You can pick up on that because you share ties with that person, and those ties make it possible to communicate with others physically and spiritually, too. These ties provide a connection that supersedes the physical world and its rules about how communication happens. This bond is often emotional, and it goes beyond life and death. Those who wish to reach out to spirits may want to reach out to their loved ones who aren't with them anymore. Spirits often try to reach out to us because they'd love to connect, too, whether to protect their loved ones, provide for them, comfort them, or just to say "Hi." The truth about life is that it goes on forever. Death is not the end, but a transition, which means it doesn't exist in the way we often think.

What Are Spirits?

What are spirits? Knowing how to define them will provide the framework you can use to reach out to them. Merriam-Webster defines a spirit as *"An animating or vital principle held to give life to physical organisms," "a supernatural being or essence," "the immaterial intelligence of the sentient part of a person," "the activating or essential principle influencing a person," or "the feeling, quality, or disposition characterizing something."*

When we talk about a spirit, we're talking about a consciousness that has transitioned from this world but is still alive. Additionally, it's a consciousness that can access the physical world and manipulate it in ways we can't see or understand, sometimes because even they do not understand it themselves. Because of this, many who work with spirits find it easier to think of them as "energy" rather than actual people because, in some ways, they think of them as being psychic projections of the dead.

Some spirits will remain on Earth because they don't realize that they're dead, while others will stick around because they want to be close to their loved ones or perhaps do some haunting. Some spirits can be benevolent and protective, while others are more malicious and dangerous. The reasons they behave in the way they do vary from spirit to spirit, but one thing remains constant. We must learn to listen and communicate with them to understand them better, which can ultimately lead us to a better understanding of death itself.

Some people hear the word spirit and immediately think about Casper, the friendly ghost, or something like that. Others think of a barely visible image that tends to hover just outside the realms of our ordinary five senses. While this is closer to the truth, that's not the whole picture. Everywhere, there are spirits. You've likely got a few around you right now. Some people are so gifted they can touch, hear, and see the spirits very clearly. Sometimes, you may spot a spirit from the corner of your eye when you're not looking right at it.

Types of Spirits

While many are scared of spirits, most of them are harmless. The only reason hauntings are considered scary is because of how they've been framed. Hauntings are simply situations where a spirit being is stuck in this realm because they have some unfinished business to handle. That said, you should note that not all spirits are human spirits. Knowing who and what you're connecting with is important to be safe and make the most of your interactions with these otherworldly beings is important. There are many kinds of spirits and other spiritual beings like entities. Let's take a look at each kind:

Ancestral spirits are your ancestors' spirits. These spirits will stick around because of the connection you share by blood. Sometimes you may have an ancestral spirit you met in person during their lifetime, and at other times you'll have ancestral spirits you never knew because they're from many generations before. You'll notice that ancestral spirits love nothing more than hanging around with family and are eager to connect with you so you can work together. They're lovely spirits to reach out to if you're just starting your spiritual path. This is because they're generally safe, and they'll keep you out of trouble.

Some spirits could cause you harm, but your ancestors usually have your back. It's not easy to have clear, proper boundaries when you're a newbie at spiritual work, so you should choose to work with your ancestors first, before any other kind of spirit. You may reach out to them and ask if they'd be interested in connecting with you and working together. Ancestral spirits can help you with your craft if you're a witch, as they can boost your powers and spells. They'll always be there to give you their assistance, and since you're their blood, you can expect that your spells will be powerful when you invoke them. Ancestral spirits will come to you in a way you can't miss. Don't be surprised if they appear in your dreams, looking much younger than the last time you met them while they were alive (if you did).

Earthbound spirits are like ancestral spirits in that they once lived on the earth. Mostly, they're here because they're still energetically connected to something that happened on earth or to a specific spot. They're the ones behind the harmless hauntings you know about. They often wind up here because they're stuck, and if their death was traumatic, they might just decide to remain around the death scene because it's not easy for them to let go of the hurt and pain inside. At other times, they stick around because they have some business they have to handle. Some spirits have passed on but don't realize their time on Earth is over, so they just hang around. They'll need a medium's help to set them free. Note that some spirits aren't stuck but simply want to pay Earth a visit.

Some spirits are considered scary, but in reality, they're the tormented spirits that are still bound to Earth and may not even know that they're being a menace to anyone. So you should have that in the back of your mind if you ever have any reason to deal with one.

Dead spirits are the same as ancestral spirits, but they're not connected to your bloodline. There are specific people that spirits of the dead like to hang around. For instance, the spirit of her deceased father may haunt a woman just because he wants to say hello, keep her safe, or provide for her. These spirits may also be earthbound. Sometimes they're not, meaning they can show up now and then just to keep track of what's happening here. For the most part, the spirits of the dead aren't dangerous. They just happen to know who you are and want to reach out.

If you notice a malevolent spirit, remember that you may be witnessing an earthbound spirit dealing with its trauma or a recording (more on that later). For the most part, spirits who hurt others are only doing so because they're in pain and unaware of it. Since there are good and bad people, it stands to reason that some spirits will have malicious intent. In this case, you need to realize that you have more power than they do on this plain, which means they have to use a lot of energy to move things around, even if you could move things easily. If you're troubled by a spirit, you must do a cleansing, and you'll be just fine.

Spirit guides are meant to help you. They tend to be around you and are willing to give you all the guidance and advice you need. Your spirit guide could be an ancestral spirit, souls you have never known, angels, or ascended masters. Everyone has several guides assigned to them once they're born, and these guides can be changed to suit the phase of the person's life. You can also be specific about reaching out to a guide to help you with money.

Some witchcraft practitioners believe that you can have both negative and positive spirit guides, and both are necessary depending on what you want to accomplish. However, it would be best if you decided to focus on only getting the spirit guides who are good for your highest purpose and the best version of your life, which is yet to come.

Plant spirits are the spirits that are connected to the plants around you. You have to recognize that these spirits are real if you work with them, so if you aren't connected to them, the odds are you're just interacting with the physical aspect of the plant and not the spiritual side of it, which would be pointless. Plant spirits are safe, and their energy is gentle. As you become more aware of plant spirits, you'll find that each has its personality, needs, and desires. The best ones to interact with are the ones in your home or space, so you can be exposed to them enough to develop rapport with the plants. You may speak to them like their spirits are listening because they are. When you begin speaking with them, you activate them spiritually. So, take time to ask them if they'd like some more water, better placement in the sun, and so on. Pay attention to whether its spirit is outgoing or calm and gentle. If you don't have psychic abilities, this may be hard, but you can work with your intuition by choosing to trust it.

Mineral spirits aren't really common. Admittedly, they're not the rock stars of the spirit group, but you'll find they're everywhere. If you have stones, minerals, and crystals around you, the odds are you have mineral spirits with you. There are many of these spirits, as many as there are crystals and stones. You can reach out to them with your intuition, among other tools which will be covered later in this book.

Mineral spirits are interested in working with you on various aspects of your life. For instance, a mineral spirit may have relationships as its specialty, while another may be good for your mental health. These spirits love to connect with living humans, but for them, it is important that they are respected. So, you could ask them what they need so you can provide them. Note that certain spirits may not be interested in working with each other. When that happens, they're not pleased about having been sprung free from the Earth. In this case, you need to put the mineral back where you found it or somewhere which resembles it.

Negative entities are bad news, and you should avoid them at all costs by not seeking them out in the first place. These are parasitic beings, sucking all the energy they can get from you. These entities are not human. Some entities will latch on to you to get an energy boost before they take off. Other entities stick to you for a long time, feeding on your energy. When you notice you have these entities, you'll also find you feel depressed, angry, confused, and empty. There are many forms of negative entities, but they all have one thing in common. They are energy thieves that stubbornly latch on to you, refusing to let go. These are some of the most common ones:

- Energy vampires
- Black spirals
- Geopathic entities
- Henchmen
- Demons
- Negative ETs
- Disincarnates
- Witches or Warlocks
- Poltergeists
- Grays

Some of these entities exist as actual beings. The others play out as build-ups of energy with no sense of consciousness. Note that meditation, visualization, and other tools can eliminate negative entities. That said, knowing when these entities connect themselves to you is for the best. They'll come for you when you're doing something low-vibrational, and they're also drawn to you when you're with people with negative entities around them. You might also notice that when you're going through something traumatizing, a toxic relationship, or a difficult situation, you'll likely have entities wanting to hang out with you. They don't do physical damage, and you may be unaware of their presence, but they'll always affect your mind and energy, and soon enough, you'll be out of both if you don't cleanse yourself of them.

Goetic demons aren't actually demonic and can be helpful if you want to work with them. In fact, most witches are happy to have their assistance. The Lesser Key of Solomon talks about 72 of them. Each one has a specific skill. For instance, one is great with love, another with money, and so on. Note that these beings aren't the spirits of actual people, but instead, they are made up of the energetic signatures of different beings. Usually, they will help you with spells, but they want you to give them something. This means that you must beware of how you negotiate with them before giving them what they want.

Once more, these Goetic demons don't cause trouble unless and until you've summoned them. If you've got problems with a spirit, note that the Goetic demons are most likely blameless in the whole thing.

The Fae are spirits in another dimension not far from our own realm, which means you can physically reach out to them. It's easier to connect with the Fae than with other forms of spirits. Many shy away from seeking the Fae's assistance, but they can be helpful. For the most part, they are bound to specific locations. If you find one along your path, the odds are the spirit won't follow you back home unless your home is actually at the same location. The Otherworld is the world of the Fae, and there are various kinds of Fae you could work with. Working with them is safe as long as you do your homework first. Just because a being is spiritual doesn't mean they automatically owe you help. The Fae are like people too. There are good ones and bad ones, and shades of gray. You can't keep them away from your home if you upset them.

Elementals are the spirits that animate the elements of fire, air, water, and earth. They're meant to help protect nature and their element. Every tree has its own spirit, and the same goes for every body of water. The odds are you've got elemental spirits outside your home right now. Some traditions state that each element has proper gods and guardians. Some spirits are also meant to take care of specific aspects of nature. For instance, the Gnomes of the Fae kingdom are earth elementals. Salamanders are fire elementals, while undines are water elementals. Air elementals are called sylphs. When working with certain elements, ask for the help of the associated elemental.

Deities are the gods and goddesses of every religion and tradition who dwell in other realms. They can work with you depending on things like which religion you resonate with and so on. Before working with deities, you'll need to research them to know which ones you resonate with. You should also ensure that you're prepared for their energy as they're really powerful, and whatever you experience will be entirely up to them. This is why you need to dive deeply into each deity you'd like to work with before you invite them into your life. Another good way to choose a deity is to set the intention that you want to work with the best deity for you and your goals and then keep your eyes peeled so you can see the signs that tell you who your deity is. You should make offerings to them regularly to keep your connection strong when you do come to know the entity.

Angels are the spirits that many people work with. Many types of myths surround these wonderful beings, and they have much more knowledge than most other beings, such as ancestral or dead spirits. The power and might of an angel should not be underestimated. In fact, you may never be able to fully comprehend the extent of their power. The thing about angels is that they think in black and white and are particular about what they consider good or bad. Research their mythology before you work with them, and learn about how they're viewed through different religions and cultures.

Demons are the last on this list, and they've always seemed scary when they're really not. Where angels are organized, demons aren't. An angel has a specific task, while a demon doesn't. Also, you should note that a demon's chaotic energy doesn't mean it's an evil entity. It just means that it's hard to predict what will come next when you work with them. There are other demons besides the Goetic ones. If you're a chaos witch, you'll want to work with demons since there's power in the chaos. Note that these beings aren't evil and are not good either. They have no bias and can bend either way. Some of them love to work with humans, but at a cost, of course. You need to be sure of what you're negotiating with them so that you're both okay with the final agreement. Note that there are demons that can be bad and terrifying, but this doesn't mean they're all like that. In fact, the Fae, angels, some ancestors, and other kinds of spirits can be scary, too. So ensure that you're protected when you work with them and be clear about what you desire before you call upon a demon.

The odds are a demon won't come to you if you don't reach out to them, so if you sense some negative being in your home and you haven't summoned them, you may be dealing with something else. Generally speaking, it's much more sensible to be careful with other entities rather than with demons. However, that doesn't mean that you should ignore just how powerful these beings are. Some of them can also exert physical power and move large things to hurt you. It's best not to summon them because they're not easy to get rid of when you've finished working with them, so you need to be good about cleansing your space and warding them off. You should also know how to work with banishing spells before you call the demons, so you can eliminate them if needed. This is a good thing to do unless you're dealing with other kinds of spirits who are loving and kind.

A Brief History of Spiritual Communication

Spiritualism became a religion that took the world by storm, and communicating with spirits through mediumship was popular in the United Kingdom and the United States. Mediumship begins with the Witch of Endor's story. The witch of Endor was also a medium who had brought the spirit of a dead prophet named Samuel back to life so that Saul, the Hebrew king, could ask him some questions. Around the early '80s, some scientists looked into Spiritualism and soon converted. While some frauds used magic tricks to make people believe they were in touch with spirits, there were some genuine mediums.

Spirit Communication Today

A study by Julie Beiscel and Gary E Schwartz demonstrated that some mediums can get accurate information about those who have passed on. Another study with at least 1,000 participants over eight years found that some humans can predict the future. The results of this study were published in the paper Feeling the future: Experimental evidence for anomalous retroactive influences on cognition and affect" by Daryl Bem in 2011.

Frequently Asked Questions

What is spirit communication?

Spirit communication is also known as mediumship. It is the spiritual practice of communicating with the spirit world. Practitioners are known as mediums, and they use tools such as tarot cards, pendulums, and often writing to perform readings from spirits that have crossed over into the living world in physical or non-physical forms, as well as other spirit beings. Mediums typically receive messages about what spiritual lessons we should take away from these past lives to help us grow spiritually in this life and prepare for our next existence. Mediums also assist spirits in preparing to pass on, so they may move on to a better place.

Where do spirits go after death?

Spirits continue to exist and evolve after the death of their bodies. Many move into a non-physical or spiritual realm called heaven or the spirit world. A medium often speaks with spirits who have passed over to this world from ours. Sometimes they remain in the astral world that overlaps ours, which is why we may dream about them or sense their presence sometimes, even if we can't see them.

What does the afterlife look like?

There are many different ideas about what the afterlife looks like. Many believe that it is a place of peace, happiness, and learning for those who have passed over, and it may be an eternal return to the world we knew before or one where we create something entirely new. The afterlife could also simply be the next phase of life in the soul's evolution that has moved on. In other words, it's their next incarnation.

Can anyone talk to spirits?

Yes. Anyone can learn how to do mediumship. It is a skill you can learn, and you don't have to be "gifted" to do it. You need to learn the techniques and access your innate mediumistic abilities.

How long does it take to learn mediumship?

It all depends on how much you want to learn and how much time you want to devote to it. There are many different ways to learn and practice this skill, so it is not like riding a bike. So, choose the right path if you want to learn the art of mediumship and how to connect with the spirit world. Just select the tool that you can relate to the most.

How do I become a medium?

You can learn mediumship by attending classes or groups, reading books, and practicing independently. There are many ways to practice and learn to communicate with people's spirits. Many people learn intuitively or through visits from spirit guides in dreams or visions. The idea is to open up your mind and heart to the possibilities of the afterlife, so you can communicate with those who have passed over. Reading this book is a great start.

Will I get in trouble for contacting spirits?

No, you are not breaking any laws by contacting spirits. Most people open themselves up to mediumship to connect with their loved ones who have passed on. There's nothing wrong with that.

Is communicating with spirits safe?

Yes, it is safe and a very positive experience. It can be a way to establish a line of communication with the spirit world. In some cases, spirits may also use mediums as messengers for those who have passed on, which can be very rewarding.

Chapter 2: Tapping into Your Psychic Abilities

We live in a day and age where many of us seek guidance. Whether it be about managing careers, relationships, illnesses, or simply how to live our lives more intentionally, finding answers from traditional sources can lead you on a long winding journey of frustration and uncertainty. We have turned away from religion, lost faith in government officials and doctors, and relied on science for all the answers. But what if there was something else? What if you could contact those who hold the answers in the spirit realm? What if they could give you clear answers, guidance, and direction? You can get all that and more if you want. All you need to do is work with your psychic senses. There are four psychic abilities known as the four clairs. These are:

Clairvoyance refers to the ability to "see clearly."
https://www.pexels.com/photo/a-woman-holding-a-locket-7278743/

- Clairvoyance
- Clairaudience
- Clairsentience
- Claircognizance

Every clair is considered extra sensory perception, or ESP, because they're supposed to be extensions of our five senses. Some psychics and occultists have different ideas. They believe that the physical senses aren't the root of the extrasensory senses but are instead a physical manifestation that comes from the psychic senses. It's not easy to prove this theory, but it does line up with a post-materialist perspective, which holds that everything springs from consciousness, and without consciousness, nothing would exist. Note that other clairs exist besides these four, but these are the most common ones.

Clairvoyance

Clairvoyance is a term that is sometimes used to refer to every psychic ability under the sun, but it really refers to the ability to "see clearly." It is the ability to perceive events and images at a distance and through time. Sometimes, it's considered an extension of regular eyesight.

In light of the view that all things come from consciousness, one could assume that means everyone is clairvoyant. Most people have their first taste of clairvoyance in childhood, while others come across this ability as grown-ups. All around you are subtle energies that you may not be aware of all the time, but that doesn't mean you don't interact with them. Those with very strong clairvoyance will likely perceive these energies easily, without training or effort. Generally speaking, the clairvoyant ability is accessible to one and all and may lie dormant in you. You can reactivate this ability. For instance, you can practice seeing and reading auras, subtle energies surrounding all living objects and beings.

Clairvoyance has a lot to do with all sorts of experiences that involve the extended abilities of sight. Also, there is inner clairvoyance and outer clairvoyance. The latter version of this ability lets you see the energies and spirits as an overlay over your physical space, as is the case with those who can see the physical manifestation of spirits. Think of it like augmented reality. External clairvoyance lets you see the spirits so clearly that they're as real as any other regular person around you. Sometimes, the beings are seen not as clear manifestations but as shadows that move, sparks of light, glowing orbs, and so on. The ability to perceive any realm besides the physical one and subtle energies using just the eyes is a form of external clairvoyance.

Then there's the matter of inner clairvoyance. Here, you see things with your mind's eye. It's almost like imagination, except you're not necessarily manipulating images you get as you may have if you were daydreaming. You see things on the viewing screen of your mind. Examples of inner clairvoyance include psychic dreams, remote viewing, precognition, and premonition.

> **Martin's story:** *"I remember having strange visions from when I was four. When I was about seven, my mom and dad took me on a trip to visit some friends of theirs in Lagos, Nigeria. As soon as I walked into their yard, I looked at the house, and what I saw was inexplicable and frightening. The house was crumbling and caving in, and I kept wondering why my parents were trying to get me to enter. I kept saying, "The house is falling." and freaking out, but they calmed me down and took me in anyway, and as soon as I walked through the front door, everything seemed normal. We left two weeks later. I still remember my father being on the phone with his friend as he exclaimed, "No," My mother, curious, asked him what the matter was. It turned out their friends' home had collapsed a month later. Fortunately, they made it out okay. I've never forgotten that experience. After that, I remember thinking I don't want to see things before they happen anymore.*

Clairvoyance, or Just Imagining?

You need to be able to tell the difference between what you imagine versus what's an actual message from spirits through your clairvoyance. When you get images from spirits, you're not the one in charge of what you see. You can't bend or twist the information to show you something else. It will just flash in your mind's eye without you trying to make it happen. If you feel any force or effort on your part when you see images in your mind's eye, the odds are you're only imagining.

How to Develop Clairvoyance

Work with Your Visualization and Imagination More

Whenever you use your imagination, you awaken your clairvoyant ability. This is because your imagination or mind's eye is the medium through which you receive the images you get. The better you are at imagining, the easier it will be for you to develop your clairvoyance.

Visualize Your Third Eye

Imagine having a third eye that sits right above and between both eyes. You already do have a third eye, even though you may not be able to see it. In this visualization exercise, you'll imagine that this third eye is closed. Then, imagine the eyelid opening up slowly. This visualization exercise aims to help you bring your intention to your subconscious mind that you'd like to awaken your dormant clairvoyance. When you do this exercise regularly for at least five to ten minutes a day, you fuel your intention with energy, and this will cause your actual third eye to follow your lead.

Work with Crystals

You can go to bed with a lapis lazuli crystal or an amethyst beneath your pillow, with the intention that you'll awaken your psychic abilities. You can also place the crystal where your third eye is located so that it can awaken this inner vision that is yours. Note that there may be other crystals you're drawn to for this purpose, so you should simply follow whatever pulls you.

Begin with the Eyes Closed

When it comes to developing clairvoyance, you may find that inner clairvoyance is much easier to begin with than outer clairvoyance. So you should close your eyes for at least five to ten minutes a day and then state your intention out loud or quietly to yourself that you're open to seeing whatever the spirit you're working with thinks is important for you to see.

Use Affirmations

You can work with affirmations, like "I am extremely clairvoyant," to help you. To do this, you can just sit comfortably, close your eyes, and repeat this to yourself with conviction for at least ten to fifteen minutes. Your mind may argue with you, but this isn't the time to be reasonable or rational. Just trust that your words will dictate your experience. If you want even more powerful affirmations, you can phrase them as though they're already a thing of the past. In other words, you could affirm any of the following:

- How did I become so clairvoyant? (This is an "affirmation.")
- I remember when I wasn't clairvoyant. Now I see everything.
- It's amazing how much better I've become at clairvoyance.

You may work with these affirmations or phrase them however you see fit.

Practice Meditation Every Day

Something about the practice of sitting in silent observation of your breath for anywhere from five to fifteen minutes each day can powerfully awaken your dormant abilities. Make sure you wear something comfortable and are free from distractions. Ask not to be disturbed if you don't live alone. Then bring your attention to your breath as you close your eyes. Breathe in through your nostrils and out through slightly parted lips. As you do this, your attention will wander away from your breath. This is fine. Simply notice and bring your attention back to your breath as often as it happens, and never beat yourself up for getting distracted. The whole point of the exercise is to awaken you to the subtle energies around you, help you channel your attention where you want it to be, and open you up to the messages that spirits around you may have for you.

Clairaudience

Clairaudience is "clear hearing," which means it's about being able to hear spirits. Sometimes it's the little voice you hear inside you when you're about to do something or go somewhere you shouldn't or when you're being led to something that will help you tremendously in life. At other times, it's quite loud and clear, often freezing you in your tracks and not giving you the time or capacity to question it. This voice reaches out to you when you have to make an important decision that could alter your life for better or worse. If you're not naturally clairaudient, you can work on this. If you are, the odds are that most of your messages come to you from your Higher Self and other spirits through this means. You'll get messages through songs, words, sounds, and more. The messages could come from within or from without. You may also experience hearing the spirits as you go to bed, wake up, or dream.

Clairaudients naturally hear more than the average person. Those who don't like loud sounds are likely clairaudients, even though they may not be aware of it because they're more sensitive to sounds than others. Clairaudients also tend to experience ringing in the ears, and no, it's not tinnitus. They get this ringing or loud-pitched tone in their ears because spirits ask them to pay attention to the moment or tune in to their inner hearing and listen.

Some of the most clairaudient people are musicians or musically inclined. Many of them hear melodious songs within themselves, or they have dreams of melodies they know they could not have come up with before putting them on paper. If you want to develop this ability yourself, you need to begin working more consciously with your hearing so you can fine-tune it.

> ***Charity's story:*** *"I had often wondered about my husband's behavior toward me in the days leading up to what I call "the end." I remember I couldn't put my finger on what was wrong, and talking to him wasn't resolving things. He wasn't doing anything I could point out was wrong, and I wondered for a while if I was being paranoid. Fed up with the feeling that way, I wanted the feeling to stop, so I reached out to my guide for help that night. The next day, while he was out at work and I was working at home, I heard a very clear message in my mind: "Go and log into the old laptop your husband abandoned two months ago." I grabbed the thing and fired it up. I never knew his password or asked, so I sat there staring at the screen, confused. Then I got a word: "Novia." I had never heard that word before but decided to type it in. I was flabbergasted by the fact that the password actually worked. This voice showed me many things I had no idea were happening under my roof. I found out that my husband had been cheating on me. He had been unfaithful to me for more than two years and had planned to leave me in a couple of months. I was finally free and happy.*

How to Develop Clairaudience

Pay Attention to the Sounds around You

When you go to bed each night, lie in the dark and pay attention to what you can hear. You should do this at night because it's easier to make it a habit when you attach it to something you have to do every day; you *can't get by without sleep*, so bedtime is a good time to practice this. Pay attention to every sound from near and far. Usually, when you need to focus on something or want to sleep, you'll tune out these sounds. You should start doing the opposite. As you do this, notice every sound that makes up the general noise you can hear. Some are more subtle than others. Practicing this for a week can give you mind-blowing results.

Keep Your Mind Attuned to Clairaudient Messages

All you have to do is visualize a radio. Turn it on. Assume that one of the stations you can get with that radio is your intuition, your ancestor spirits, or whatever else you may want to connect to. Envision yourself tuning in to that frequency. If you want, imagine this brings your spirit guides around a table with you, ready to answer any questions you may have. Notice if you're picking up on any message from them. Sometimes, the voices that come through will be very clear so that you know exactly what they're saying. Sometimes, hearing them may not be easy, or you may get nothing. If that's the case, that's not enough reason to give up. Continue this practice, and you'll find yourself doing better at picking up clairaudient messages.

Practice Meditation Daily

Like all other clairs, this ability can be honed by sitting in silence daily. Remember, you don't need more than fifteen minutes.

Use Affirmations

You can do this right after your meditation session so that you're in a receptive mode to the suggestions you're giving your subconscious mind. You can use the following affirmations:

- *I clearly hear what spirits have to say to me all the time*
- *I remember when I couldn't hear a thing from spirits. Now it's every day.*
- *My clairaudient ability is at its peak*

My inner ears are always open to what spirits have to say Other things that can help you develop this ability are:

1. Set a clear intention that you want to use this ability. Writing it down makes it more likely to happen.
2. Choose not to be afraid of whatever you hear, good or bad. Being afraid is a good way to block your clairaudience, as your Higher Self isn't interested in spooking you unnecessarily.
3. Use binaural beats on the Internet to help you become more clairaudient.

Clairsentience

Clairsentience is "clear-feeling." This is a very grouped gift and one that is used by many people daily. It's basically letting your feelings guide you.

For instance, you may feel off at the moment, and then you decide to step away from where you are on the curb, only for an accident to happen right where you were standing moments ago. Or you may feel weird and then turn around to find that it's because someone has been staring at you long and hard.

Clairsentient messages come to you through gut feelings, empathy, and physical sensations. When it comes to your gut feelings, those are strong emotions you get that you can almost feel physically in your body. Think of intense fear or excitement. You know your actions are right when you feel good in your gut. When you get sick, you know how to get out of your situation or stop dealing with something. If you paid more attention to your gut, you'd probably be in less trouble than you are now.

Empathy is what lets you know how others are feeling or what it's like to be them. It makes it easy to experience life as someone else – but if you're not careful, you may have trouble telling which emotions are yours and which aren't, especially if you're an empath. When it comes to clairsentience through physical sensations, you may notice a tingle along your spine, a shiver, a change in air pressure or temperature, or tickling. These are just some of the sensations you get as you connect with the spirits through clairsentience.

__Lulu's story:__ "It's a funny thing, but when I'm about to make a decision about something, I get really uncomfortable prickly sensations in my body when it's a bad decision, and when it's a good one, the top of my head feels like cool air's blowing on it. The one time I disregarded this and went ahead with something I was getting prickles about; it didn't work out. Lesson learned."

How to Develop Clairsentience

Read Other People's Energies

Ask a good friend to get a picture of someone they know who you don't know at all. Look at the person's eyes in the picture to get a lock on their energy. Is it positive or negative? Ask yourself questions about this person, like what they're like as a person. Ask yourself if you can pick up anything from their eyes, and then let your friend know your findings. Your friend should let you know if you were spot on or not. Try this as often as possible until you get better at it.

Practice Psychometry

This is an exercise where you'll get an object that belongs to someone. It's got to be something the person has worn often, as the more you wear something, the more it absorbs your energy. As you develop your clairsentience, you should be able to read the residual energy from objects. Hold the item in your hands for a minute or more, and notice if you're picking up on positive or negative energy.

Pay Attention to Your Chakras

In this exercise, you'll connect with your own energy centers and read the energy you give off. You should learn about chakras first before you do this exercise. This is a good exercise because you'll learn more about how you feel and what emotions you embody every time you do this. Sit or lie in a comfortable position, and then begin with the first or root chakra. In your mind's eye, see it as a colored wheel or orb of light that spins, and let the light extend outside of your body by at least a few inches. Then check how you feel about the chakra, and notice what emotions come up. You may also notice certain sensations in your body that will let you know how you're really doing in life.

Claircognizance

Claircognizance is "clear-knowing." If you're claircognizant, you have a way of knowing things you shouldn't know without anyone telling you. You get the information in thought form from the spirits you interact with. Sometimes, it's just a thought, and at other times you get blocks of thoughts called "downloads" because it seems like they're downloaded into your mind. You may have inspired ideas about situations, people, and places. The claircognizant often strongly believes that what they know is true, even though they cannot logically say why. Often, the information they get turns out to be accurate.

Claircognizants tend to love working with their minds a lot. They're mentally talented people who love to analyze things and break them down in their minds. These people are excellent problem solvers and good at seeing the connections between things that others would miss. These people had an answer for everything, even when they were children, and were probably snubbed for being "know-it-alls." This ability isn't well-known, as more people know clairaudience and clairvoyance. Just because this power is subtle doesn't mean that it's not effective and powerful. Claircognizance can express itself through automatic writing and channeling, as well. You may get a truly amazing idea, or you somehow know how something will work out. You might get the sense that someone is being dishonest, or you know you should pass up an opportunity because something about it is off and not good for you. In those cases, you may have experienced claircognizance.

The difference between claircognizance and your thoughts is that your conscious mind cannot control your claircognizant messages. It can only witness the information. With claircognizance, if you trust your ability, the odds are you'll never question a claircognizant message. Also, your recurring thoughts are rooted in the ego, and the ego works to keep you safe from being disappointed, embarrassed, or from failing. Claircognizance is beyond the ego and is rooted in wisdom. It also demands that you act on the information based on faith.

> **Hailey's story:** *"I've noticed that whenever I'm confused about something or it stresses me out, all I have to do is decide that the answers and solutions will come to me when they're ready and then forget about the problem. I'll get struck by an idea to handle the problem a certain way, and it's usually the right call. There have also been times when I was supposed to be part of something I've always wanted to participate in, only to wake up in the morning with a strong knowledge that I shouldn't leave my home. I usually end up seeing why following that knowledge was a good idea later on. Either I hear the event I was supposed to go to didn't happen, or I find out that there's something better and easier lined up for me.*

How to Develop Claircognizance

Practice automatic writing

This is a good way to improve your claircognizance. Get a piece of paper or start a new document on your computer. Tell the spirit you're working with that you'd like to reach out to them. You can ask them questions or let them speak to you about whatever they want. When you write, don't think. Just note whatever first comes into your mind, even if it seems gibberish or doesn't make sense initially. Don't judge it, don't question it, and have no expectations about what the message may be. Your conscious mind is only there to be a witness, not to control things. You may get nonsense the first few attempts, but after a while, some golden nuggets will begin to flow through you. With time and practice, you won't need to sit for too long before information begins to flow.

Set the Intention to Be More Claircognizant

Write your intention down somewhere you can see it. You can write it down first thing in the morning and the last thing at night, too.

Set Time Aside to Receive Messages from Your Intuition or Spirit

You can do this after meditation, so you'll have a mind more conducive to knowing what you need.

Work with Your Crown Chakra

This chakra is on top of your head. Imagine a vortex with white light that spins on top of your head. Feel it open up, using your imagination. Imagine a stream of light flowing in through that energy center. The stream of light is spiritual knowledge and wisdom. Then frame your questions in your mind, and sit and wait for the answers to come through. Practice this daily for the best results.

Chapter 3: Getting Ready for Spirit Work

You know the saying, "Proper preparation prevents poor performance." So, this chapter is dedicated to everything you need to know about how to prepare for your spiritual journey. You can't just decide to start working with spirits without laying the groundwork for success first - which means getting your mind, body, and spirit ready for the task ahead. If you don't take time to do the prep work, you may encounter difficulties along the way. For instance, you may have trouble establishing a clear connection with the spirit you want to reach. Even worse, you may attract the attention of spiritual beings you want to avoid at all costs. You may also find that each session you spend communicating with spirits tends to leave you drained and out of sorts. If that's the case, it can be difficult to enjoy the practice, let alone keep going with it, and you may miss out on all sorts of good things.

Before doing any spiritual work, you must ground yourself.
https://www.pexels.com/photo/women-holding-hands-at-a-table-with-burning-candles-7267684/

What Is Grounding?

Grounding connects you to the Earth's energy. What's the theory? It's believed that the Earth transmits reliable and grounded energy, a resource for dealing with difficult times. Who can ground themselves? Anyone can use grounding to eliminate negative energy in their body so they can feel better and be more open to the subtle energies of the spirit world. Also, it helps to get you in the right mindset for the work ahead of you.

Before doing any spiritual work, you must ground yourself because the spiritual mediumship and development process can raise your energy levels to unhealthy heights. And since you'll be helping spirits with their business, you don't want any energy-related illnesses like high blood pressure, headaches, or dizziness. Also, you don't want to create a situation where you're so carried away by the spiritual work that you no longer handle the mundane, day-to-day stuff that you should.

A Grounding Meditation

This is a meditation used to center your energy. If you have never meditated before, find a quiet space where you can relax and will not be interrupted. You may keep your eyes open or closed, but it is recommended that you keep them closed. You can lie on the ground, sit on it, or sit on a chair but make sure your feet are bare and firmly planted on the floor beneath you.

Lightly rest your hands on your stomach (or on the surface of your yoga mat or surface surrounding you). Remember that your intentions are the most important factor in this ritual, so if you want to feel lighter, more present, or more energetic, don't just focus on the breathing but the intention. Begin to breathe slowly in through your nostrils and out through your slightly parted lips.

Imagine a powerful red light coming up through the earth and into your body wherever it connects with the floor. Let this light either bring you the energy you need or take away what you don't need. For the former, see energy moving from the earth into your body. For the latter, see your body's chaotic energy in the form of black smoke moving into the earth to be absorbed by its red light. If you're not good at visualization, you can imagine the feeling of the energy flowing in the direction you want it to. Keep going until you feel focused and grounded.

Clearing Your Mind

Before doing spirit work, your mind has to be clear so you can focus on the only thing that matters; the intention you have for the work you're about to do. You can't escape your mind, so you should do your best to keep it clear and free because that's how you get the best results when working with spirits. The following are things you can do to clear your mind for the task ahead.

Write Down Your Feelings or Thoughts as They Come Up

Sometimes, we tend to change our minds so quickly that we don't even realize how mad or sad we can get until it's too late and we meditate in a bad mood. By writing it down before meditating, you can analyze your feelings, possibly discovering that they are not simply based on a current situation but something deeper.

Go for a Walk in Nature

One lovely thing to do is to go for a walk by the river. When you're out in nature, you can feel the spirits around you, and when you go for a walk by the river, trees, or in the sunlight, it just seems so much more like you're in your natural element. Nothing is better than getting fresh air and walking among trees and grass. There's also nothing that gives you more peace than feeling at one with nature while taking time out of your schedule to get away from society and just be with yourself.

Meditate on the Spiritual Aspect of the Problem

Sometimes, we get so wrapped up in the idea that we need to keep busy with our lives that we forget about spirituality. If you are feeling overwhelmed, then first ask yourself if your life is going according to what you set out to do or if there's something else you wanted to do that somehow fell off your schedule. If it isn't, ask yourself what it is you want and how you can live in a way that doesn't cause stress. If it is simply a matter of being too busy and not spending enough time with your family or friends or doing whatever activities are important to you due to obligations from school or work etc., then ask yourself, have you done everything that you can to make things work? And if the answer is no, then it's time to re-evaluate how your life is going.

Meditate to Help You Find What You Need

Sometimes, it's hard to have a clear mind if you're struggling with stress and other issues in life. Most people who want to meditate want to get rid of their stress. At least for the short term. But it's important to understand that meditation isn't about getting rid of anything. It's about finding out what you need. Stress is a result of unaddressed needs. The first step is usually coming to terms with your situation for the time being, but after that, you have to ask yourself what you need to do to find strength and grow as a person. Sometimes it is pretty clear, sometimes not. For example, if you feel like life is going too fast and you want a break from the craziness of your life, then go ahead and take one, but if you need to find something spiritually powerful inside yourself, try meditating on it. If this seems too hard a task, try meditating to notice how you feel, so you can release what doesn't serve you.

Don't Be Afraid to Ask for Help

Don't be afraid of finding a teacher who can show you techniques that can help you clear your mind if nothing you do is working for you. Ask for whatever you need from the universe to help you along the way, and do your best to put in an honest effort. As long as you're not doing everything for yourself and contorting your energy, spirits will come through with the right form of help for you.

Raising Your Vibration

There are many exercises to raise your vibration for spiritual work, including visualization, meditation, drumming, and dancing. Let's look at a few.

Meditation: This can be done by sitting on a cushion or sofa with your eyes closed. Focus on visualizing a white light in the center of your being – which expands outwards from you into the universe. It also helps to use an object as a focal point during meditation, such as a candle or crystal ball, as your meditative focal point.

Dancing and Drumming: In these types of practices, it is recommended that you incorporate movement to achieve higher levels of awareness and consciousness. There are many videos of shamanic drumming that you can find for free on the Internet to help you to raise your vibration.

Mantras: Mantras are a great way to connect with your higher self and help to raise your vibration. There are many different types of mantras, for example, the "peace be still" mantra "Om Shalom Shanti" or the "Om Mani Padme Hum," which means "Hail to the Jewel in the Lotus."

Sharing Intentions: This practice has been used by native people to reach people they may wish to get guidance from or perhaps even just let their loved ones know that they're thinking about them. This practice can be done practically anywhere at any time. Once you've set the intention, simply speak your intention out loud and feel it in your heart.

Tuning In: This practice is used when we need to tune in to our higher self or to help us become aware of the energy of others. It is also a good way to get us in touch with our collective consciousness, which can provide guidance and inspiration. This can be done by simply tuning in using intent and focusing on the energy of your Higher Self or any spirit you want to work with.

Visualization: Visualization is a powerful practice that can help you reach different levels of consciousness and awareness. It works by helping you to see your surroundings differently by creating imagery in your mind of what you want to achieve. This could be an image of yourself holding up an energy ball towards the universe, an image of the end result you want to get from interacting with the spirits, or a scene with your spiritual guides or loved ones. Once you have this image in mind, use your intention and focus on this vision until it becomes real for you.

Positive Affirmations: Having positive affirmations is just as important as having intentions. Positive affirmations are statements about our lives that we believe to be true or want to be true. They are mostly positive statements used to help you validate yourself and your spirituality by helping to raise your vibration. Some examples of these affirmations include: "I am a Light Being" or "I am already doing the work that I need to do to achieve my goals."

Occult Symbolism and Why It Matters

What exactly is the occult? The term "occult" comes from the Latin word *occultus*, which means hidden. It was originally a term for knowledge of the supernatural that was kept secret and only passed on through the generations from master to student. The source of this information could be magical-religious in nature or not. This encompassed subjects considered taboo, such as astrology, alchemy, magic, divination, and witchcraft.

It is believed that occult knowledge originated from prehistoric religions when it served as a bridge between man and God. The ancient pagan religions had their own set of rituals and symbols that related to different elements of nature, stars, the seasons, and the cycles of life. These symbols were used to convey specific messages from the spirit world to people to understand and interpret these messages as best as possible. The knowledge about them was passed on orally from one generation to another. Later, with the expansion of literacy, written records started appearing. This was when some occult practices became more widespread and common knowledge among different societies.

Many people are interested in spirituality and ritual work but don't know much about the occult. Having a basic knowledge of what's going on is not only interesting, but it's also important. By learning more about the occult and its symbols, you'll better understand what you're working with during your rituals. You don't need to know too much, just enough to use it for personal purposes. As you learn more about them, you will also understand why and how they're used for your personal spirit work. You'll also grasp the messages that the spirits are trying to share with you even better.

One-Week Prep for Spirit Work

The following is a seven-day preparation routine to help you begin your spiritual work. When you wake up each morning or when you go to bed at night:

1. **Ground Yourself:** You're just waking up and want to be fully present. You can just sit up in bed with your feet on the floor for five minutes while you breathe consciously. Grounding yourself at the

end of the day is okay, so you can shed the energetic debris of the day.

2. **Meditate:** When you've finished grounding yourself, it's time to meditate. Do this for at least five minutes and, at most, ten minutes. You can get right into the meditation from the grounding process. This will help clear your mind and get you in the headspace needed to receive psychic communication.

3. **Visualize Your Chakras Opening Up:** If you're not good at visualizing, imagine the sensation of more energy flowing through each chakra, from the root to the crown.

4. **Affirmations**: Affirm to yourself that you're now sensitive to every good spiritual being with nothing but the best of intentions and your highest good in mind. Phrase this affirmation however you like. Don't be surprised if you begin sensing the presence around you.

5. **Fast Forward:** Now, mentally move yourself to a time in the future when you're very adept at communicating with spirits. Imagine that you just finished a session with them, and thank them. Feel deep appreciation in your heart for the clarity of their messages. Do this for five minutes.

If you don't want to do these steps all at once, you can split them however you like, so you do some when you wake up and the others when you go to bed. Do this consistently for seven days, and you'll see phenomenal results.

Chapter 4: Channeling the Spirits

Now that you've gone through the preparatory week, you're ready to start working with the spiritual realm and its inhabitants. Ideally, you should wait until you have finished reading the book before you begin your practice, especially the last chapter, which has some pertinent information you must have if you want to practice spirit work safely and powerfully. You must know how to cleanse yourself before and after work to avoid issues.

It's a known fact that the best way to dive deep into the truth of our existence is to enter into a trance state.
https://www.pexels.com/photo/a-woman-sitting-at-the-table-7278733/

In this chapter, you'll learn about getting into a trance state, the steps to enter a trance, and how you can transmit your questions and intentions to the spirits you're working with. You'll also learn the importance of closing the connection when you've finished and how to do that. Before getting into all this information, please beware of deliberately seeking out negative entities with malicious intentions. Ideally, you should have friendly spirits like your ancestors around you when you work with other spirits so that they can keep you safe in case there's any funny business from other spirits you're dealing with.

What Is a Trance State?

Going into a trance is an ancient practice. For several thousands of years, humans have used all sorts of methods to alter the state of their consciousness so they can connect with the worlds unseen. Many traditions, cultures, and religions incorporate trance states in their spiritual practices. It's a known fact that the best way to dive deep into the truth of our existence is to enter into a trance state. Regardless of your spiritual practices and beliefs, you'll find the trance state is very useful for deepening your spiritual journey. If you want to connect with spirits, you should definitely learn to get into a trance. The question is, what is that?

A trance state is a different state of mind or consciousness from your ordinary waking consciousness, which you're using to read this book. In this state, you're neither fully awake nor quite asleep. In other words, the trance state sits on the razor-thin edge between the conscious and subconscious minds. The trance state is what you achieve when you're off daydreaming or zoning out. You need to remember five levels when it comes to trance states.

Very Light Trance: This is level one. At this stage, your awareness moves to focus predominantly on what's happening inside you. At this point, you become aware of what you're thinking and how you feel physically and emotionally. If you practice meditation regularly, odds are you already know what it is like to enter this state of consciousness.

Light Trance: This is level two. You can tell you're at this level because the consciousness you experience will be akin to a dream. Think about how it feels to fantasize and get lost in worlds you created in your mind. This is what it feels like in this level of trance. If you're watching the television, reading a book, or taking a trip you've been on so often that you don't have to think hard to find your way, that means you've experienced this trance.

Medium Trance: Level three of trance states is about being in the zone. This is also known as the flow state. In this state, you're unaware of the passage of time, your surroundings, and even your body.

Deep Trance: This is level four, and you experience it when you're in the normal sleep state or having hypnagogia, which is the point where you're falling asleep and begin to witness shapes and colors that pop in and out of your mind's eye, among other sorts of images. You experience hypnagogia when your conscious mind begins to lose control and wind down for the day. You may also notice that your mind will concoct the weirdest stories at this point, and you may feel or hear hallucinations and even feel the sensation of falling even though you're lying on your bed.

Very Deep Trance: Level five is the last level. At this point, you no longer have conscious awareness. You're not even having dreams but are comatose for all intents and purposes.

Why Does Trance Matter?

When it comes to spirit work, the best levels of trance to work with are from levels two to four. You need to be in a trance state when working with spirits because this state of consciousness makes it possible to silence the critical conscious mind, which tends to interfere with spiritual communication. Put yourself into a trance first because your rational, conscious mind likes to act as an obstacle to the subconscious mind. Your ego is meant to keep you safe from anything it thinks is a threat which, according to your ego, is anything that would threaten its own existence. The problem with the ego is that it makes it tough for you to get rid of toxic habits, learn new, better ones, and go deeper in your spiritual practice because it worries you may experience a loss of ego or ego death. Your ego will use every tool to frustrate your spiritual work, including splitting, projection, denial, and repression.

Trance has always been used in spiritual work, helping people connect with their spirit guides, soul families, ancestors, and animal guides, among other beings of the spirit realm. Many theories explain how trance can help you deepen your connection with the spirit. Still, the most plausible one is that everyone's subconscious mind is connected, creating something called the Collective subconscious, a concept suggested by Carl Jung. It's also called the Deep Mind or Universal Mind. Through the Deep Mind, we can connect with any energy we want.

How to Enter a Trance State

You can use the following methods to get into a trance state, whether the light trance or the deep trance state. The way you work with these methods is up to you, but please note that if you struggle with schizoaffective disorder, schizophrenia, or any other sort of mental illness that is deeply troublesome, you should check with your medical professional first to be sure it's okay to practice these things.

Use breath work: When you breathe in a certain pattern and at a certain pace, you're likely to change your state of consciousness. There are several yogic breathing practices (breathwork) that you can use to help you. For instance, pranayama is breathwork meant to help you get rid of stumbling stones on an emotional and mental level in your life. It can also create a trance state. Try *udgeeth pranayama.* Udgeeth means "deep and rhythmic chanting," and pranayama means "breathwork," "breathing exercises," or "breath and energy mastery." With this particular form of pranayama, you'll chant the Om mantra in a rhythm. Om is pronounced like "home" but without the letter h. Here are the steps:

1. Sit somewhere comfortable, preferably on a stable surface. Keep an elongated spine. A folded blanket beneath your hips can be excellent support if you sit on the floor. Plant both feet on the floor firmly and flatly if you use a chair.
2. Close your eyes or keep a soft gaze.
3. Begin breathing deeply through the nose as you let your body relax. Check your face, neck, and shoulders to be sure you're not holding tension there.
4. As you breathe, ensure only your belly moves up and down on each inhale and exhale.
5. Do your best to ensure the exhales are longer than the inhales, and don't strain while you breathe.
6. While breathing, chant the Om and pay attention to how the mantra vibrates. Also, notice how your breath feels. You want to chant loud enough to hear yourself and feel the vibration but softly enough to remain focused on your breath simultaneously.
7. Keep chanting while you breathe slowly, and keep your attention on your breath. When you're ready to come out of it, take a moment to

sit in silence so you can absorb all you've received from the spiritual experience.

Use Mantras: A mantra is a sound or word you repeat to get into a trance. It's not the same thing as praying, which only leads to a light trance state since you'll need your conscious mind to pray. If you're drawn to prayer, you could try different ways, such as using a language you make up as you go, a different language than you're used to, and so on. Doing it this way will help you bypass your conscious, rational mind.

Try Shamanic Drumming and Sounds: Shamans work with drums because they help to put the spiritual people into a state of trance so they can begin their shamanic journeys. You could buy a little drum (like a bongo or a hand drum) or work with some shamanic drumming sounds online. The best sounds are repetitive and have no vocals. If you pick sounds with vocals, it's best to opt for something that isn't in your language and, therefore, cannot distract you. Other excellent tools to use are binaural and isochronic beats.

Look Up: This method is simple. Sit somewhere quiet and comfortable where you won't be bothered or distracted, and then look at something above your eye level. Keep your gaze fixed on that point, and as you do so, notice the walls and other objects in your peripheral vision while simultaneously maintaining your attention on the spot just above you. Hold this gaze for no less than five minutes.

Hypnotize Yourself: Self-hypnosis is an amazing tool to get into a trance and do your spiritual work. It's more powerful than most realize, and it's safe because you're the one in charge of how deeply you go into your trance, and no one can make you do anything you don't already want to do. To hypnotize yourself, stay in a dark room. Make sure all is quiet, and there will be no distractions or disturbances. Lie down and pay attention to your breath. In your mind, say to yourself over and over, "Sleep... Sleep... Deep sleep... Deep sleep..." Do this for several minutes, as slowly as possible. In time, you'll find that your body feels lighter and warmer than usual, and your mind will go completely quiet. At this point, you're in a trance.

Use a Pendulum: You can swing the pendulum back and forth in front of you to send you into a trance state. Just sit somewhere quiet and comfortable, and then move your attention to your pendulum. You can give it a gentle swing to begin its movement, or you can use the pendulum to move (it will move because of the ideomotor effect). You should do this for five to ten minutes and find yourself in a trance.

Now You're in Trance

Ideally, before getting into the trance state, you should be clear about your intentions for communicating with spirits. Here are some ideas you may want to pursue:

- You may want to ask the spirits questions about their own lives
- You may have questions about a specific situation you're dealing with in your life
- You can ask them for clarity about what to do next
- You can ask them about universal truths, such as the laws of manifestation
- You may ask the spirits to show you what you most need to know at the moment
- You can let them know you're willing to be a channel for them to speak through on your behalf or someone else's behalf
- You can request that they flow healing energy through you and to you mentally, physically, or emotionally
- You may assign them a task to help you stop someone who's frustrating you in their tracks

Whatever your intentions or questions are, have them in your mind as you slip into a trance. When you do, the next thing is to restate that intention or ask the question aloud and then sit and wait expectantly. If you've chosen to use automatic writing, you should be ready with your pen and paper. If you're channeling the spirit's answers, you'll find it useful to have the sound recorder app on your phone open and ready to go.

Some sessions don't require you to ask any questions of the spirits. In those cases, you can simply sit with them in silent communion. If it's an intention, you'll know they've decided to help you with it when you get an inner knowing or other messages from them that what you desire is a done deal. Then you can sit in appreciation for some more time or get out of trance.

Exiting the Trance State

It's not enough to know how to get into a trance. You've got to know how to get out of it too. When you've finished working with the spirits, you should thank them and let them know their presence is no longer needed — unless they're friendly spirits like your ancestors or a loved one. If they are other spirits you're unfamiliar with, you must thank them and instruct them to leave your space. After that, return your attention to your breath and allow yourself to slowly come back to consciousness by paying attention to the sounds around you, how you feel in your body, and anything else that can connect you with the material world. Feel the ground beneath your feet, notice what your mouth tastes like, and feel what it's like to be present. Finally, if you close your eyes, you can now open them. If you had them open with a soft gaze, you could slowly allow the room around you to come into focus.

Cleansing Yourself and Your Space

At the end of the spirit communication, cleaning yourself and your space is important. This is because you don't want any lingering, residual energy that could act as a magnet, attracting the spirits back to your space where they may decide to take agency and do whatever they want, which may not always be the best thing for you. So, you can't skip the process of cleansing yourself and your home or the space you communicated with the spirit. Here's how:

Use Salt Water: When you've finished with the spirit channeling and know they've gone, you may spritz yourself with salt water from a spritzer bottle. Salt can purify energy and eliminate any stale or bad energy around you. You should also spritz this water around your home. If you don't have a spritz bottle, simply make sure you have a bowl of water with some salt in it before you begin the session. Then when you've finished, you can dip your hand in the bowl of salt water and then flick your fingers over yourself to get the water on your body. Then, flick the water into the air around your space to cleanse the area. If you like, you can also take a bath with salt water and wash the clothes you used to reach out to the spirits with salt water, too.

Use an Egg: Egg cleansing is a practice that is well-known by many cultures across the world. All you have to do is take an uncooked egg and then begin to rub it against your body, starting from the crown of your head, and work your way down to your feet. Ensure you use downward strokes. It should be like pushing the energy away from your body and down to the ground. Make sure you don't bring the egg back up to any part of your body that you've already touched. When you've finished doing this, you can use the same egg to cleanse the room by walking from corner to corner with it held up in the air until you've covered the entire perimeter of your living space. Then, take the egg outside your home, and break it.

The Green Candle Method: Some people use a green candle for its cleansing properties. Just light it and walk around your space, again taking it to each corner until you've covered the whole perimeter of your living space. Then, like you used the egg cleansing method, break the green candle, which will release its energy into the atmosphere to clear your space.

A Final Note

When reaching out to the spirits through trance, you need to know that you may not have success on the first try or even the first few tries. It's important to be patient with yourself. Just continue to practice, and sooner or later, you'll begin receiving messages from the other side. Also, it has to be stated once more that you must avoid any negative entity. Don't seek them out. If someone comes to you for help reaching out to a spirit that was a bad person in their past life, the odds are you'll get an intuitive nudge not to do it. Honor that nudge every time it pops up. Also, if it turns out you're connecting with a spirit, and something feels off, close the connection immediately by telling them politely but firmly that they are to leave your space as you're closing the session right away. Don't wait for a response because you don't need their permission to end the session. End it, cleanse yourself and your space, and ask for the protection of your friendly ancestor spirits

Spirit communication can be an exciting and empowering experience. Still, it's important to ensure that you have the proper tools and knowledge to do it. If you don't have the right safety precautions, that excitement could quickly turn into anxiety or fear.

A trance state is a psychological state considered a heightened level of cognitive functioning in hypnosis where people appear more suggestible than usual. Several advantages come from entering this state before communicating with spirits. One of them is detaching the conscious mind from all external stimuli and thoughts, making for a much more pleasant overall experience. Other advantages include the following:

- **Lowering your fear and anxiety**, making it easier to stay in the moment and connect with spirits. The subconscious mind is what will be talking to spirits, so you don't want your conscious mind to interfere with or overthink it. You want your subconscious mind to be as clear and focused as possible so you can get past your initial fears of spirit communication and find the comfort level you need to get answers from those who have passed on.

- **Clearing out all doubt** in your mind about spirit communication. If you have a negative thought about spirits and spirit communication beforehand, feelings of fear, anxiety, and doubt will affect you. These thoughts are too strong to overcome by your conscious mind alone. So having that subconscious mind cleared out before hitting the ground running will make things much easier for you. This is why you should get into a trance.

Chapter 5: Spiritual Tools and How to Use Them

Some practitioners believe you shouldn't use tools to communicate with spirits, but that's not the case. If you're a beginner, you'll find the tools especially useful for your practice, as they'll make it much easier to open up a line of communication with the spirit world. There are several tools you could work with. Check each one out to find what resonates with you the best, and use only that one unless your intuition tells you it's time to try something else. Here are some of the tools:

Not only can you use the pendulum to help you diagnose energetic and spiritual problems, but you can also use it to make decisions and connect with spirits.
https://www.pexels.com/photo/close-up-shot-of-a-silver-round-pendant-7267149/

- The pendulum
- The Ouija board
- Paper and pen (for channeled or automatic writing)
- Mirror (for scrying)
- A bowl of water (for scrying)
- Candles and incense sticks (also for scrying)

No matter which tool you're working with, ensure you cleanse it with salt water or smudge it with sage. You should also charge the tools. You can do this by letting the tools sit out in the sunlight, under the full moon, or simply by placing your hands over them and envisioning or feeling good energy flowing from your hands into the tools. Now it's time to look at how to use each one.

Communicating with the Pendulum

The pendulum can be of any material. Some are just necklaces with a charm, crystal, or weighty items you can swing. The item mustn't be too heavy or too light. Preferably, it should be half an ounce. The best pendulums have a weight that tapers off into a point and is about six inches. If you don't want to buy one, you can make it yourself with any makeshift string and objects like keys as the weight. Not only can you use the pendulum to help you diagnose energetic and spiritual problems, but you can also use it to make decisions and connect with spirits. You can even use it to find things you've lost. Here's how to use a pendulum correctly.

Figure Out Its Programming

First, you want to know how your pendulum swings when it tells you yes, no, or maybe. You should ensure that no one is around to disturb or bother you while you work this out. Also, ensure that you're in the right frame of mind (not upset or tired), so you don't misinterpret your answers. Since your intention is to use the pendulum to interact with the spirit, it is best to treat your pendulum right and handle the process with reverence.

Sit at a table or a desk, and lean on it with your elbow to support it. The elbow should belong to your dominant hand. Hold the pendulum in that hand between your thumb and index finger, and let it swing on its own. Then you can ask the pendulum, "Show me yes," and wait to see which way it swings. If it doesn't swing, you've got no reply. Move on to the next request, "Show me no." This is because some pendulums prefer to answer one question first instead of the other. The pendulum may move back and forth, left and right, in big or little circles. Note its answers as you ask it. You should also ask it to show you "I don't know" and "Maybe." If you prefer, you can draw a circle on a piece of paper, split it into four quadrants, and label each quadrant "Yes," "No," "Maybe," and "I don't know."

When you've worked out the directions, ask some simple questions you already know the answers to as a warm-up to be sure that everything's working as it should.

Get Into a State of Trance

This is to put you in the vibration where you can summon the energy of the spirits you want to interact with and keep your mind focused on your intentions and questions.

Ask the Spirit If They're Present

Your pendulum should swing to let you know. You can also use your pendulum chart to find out by letting the pendulum hang over each word. Wherever it begins to move, that's your answer.

Ask the Spirit Whatever You Want to Know

Obviously, you're limited to yes and no questions unless you want to create a pendulum chart with every letter of the alphabet (in which case, perhaps an Ouija board would be more appropriate).

When you've finished, thank the spirits and close the session, then cleanse yourself, your pendulum, and your space.

Communicating through the Ouija Board

The Ouija board is an easy way to connect with spirits. Many are nervous about this board, as they think it's a portal through which malevolent forces can come. There's reason to be careful with this board, though. If you'd never leave your home door unlocked every time you went out, then you should be mindful of not ending a session properly. When you want to connect to the spirit world through the Ouija board (or any other tool), you've got to know exactly with whom you want to communicate. If you didn't like a certain person when they were alive, the odds are you're not going to want to hear from them just because they've passed on. So be clear about your intentions first. You can buy a board or make one yourself.

How to Make Your Ouija Board

1. Get a large piece of paper and write "Yes" at the top left and "No" at the top right.
2. Beneath the words "Yes" and "No," write out each letter of the alphabet in a slight arc. Let the first set of letters be from A to M and the second set be from N to Z.
3. At the bottom left-hand side of the paper, write "Hello," and at the bottom right, write "Goodbye."
4. Draw a circle above the word "Yes" and put dashes around it, so you've got a sun with rays.
5. Draw a crescent moon above the word "No" and draw rays emanating from it.
6. For the planchette, work with an upside-down glass.

Using the Ouija Board

Set the mood: The room you're using should be dark. Candlelight is a good idea, as spirits will be drawn to the flames and fire energy. Eliminate all distractions and put away all phones and other devices.

Set the board up: You can let it rest on your knees.

Do a warm-up: To warm up the board, move the planchette to form the infinity or figure of eight symbol.

Figure out who you want to connect with, then enter into a state of trance: When you know the spirit you want to reach out to, you can use whichever method is best for you to get into a trance state.

Ask them if they're present, and when they confirm, ask them your questions: When asking them questions, do your best to be polite to your guests. Note that you can get rid of them if they're rude to you, taunt you, or ruin the séance you're holding.

Write down all the messages they give you: In time, you may notice that you're starting to fill in the blanks for them because you're channeling the information in real-time and much faster than you can move the planchette. Write it all down because it will definitely prove useful information. Note that sometimes the spirits make spelling errors. That's perfectly fine.

When you're done, thank them for their time, and send them on the way: You can thank them for taking the time and effort it took them to connect with you. Then tell them to be on their way and leave your space.

Cleanse yourself and your space: Use any of the methods mentioned earlier.

Extra Tips: Don't use the Ouija board alone if you are over-excited. The odds are that if you're very excited, you may want to ask too many questions. In a group, you may confuse the spirit if everyone asks questions at once. Let this be a turn-by-turn situation.

Another tip is never to ask questions to discover things you shouldn't, like when or how you'll die. Most spirits will not give you a serious answer. Don't waste your time asking questions you've already figured out the answers to. And you want to ensure that the spirit guest with you isn't trying to take over the session because you summoned it for answers, not to be lectured into oblivion.

Just because something came through the board doesn't mean it's true, so you must check in with your gut and practice discernment to be safe. Only take what truly resonates from the message and eliminate the rest. There will be times when the séance doesn't work out. And that's fine. Spirits are like humans in that sometimes they don't feel chatty. Don't take it personally. Just try another time again.

Communicating through Automatic Writing

1. First, know what you want to get out of this interaction.
2. Clear your mind and ground yourself.
3. Get a paper and pen sheet, or open up a new document on your computer.
4. Get into a trance state.
5. Say "Hello" to the spirit, and then ask it your questions.
6. Allow your hand to write as it will. Don't judge anything you get.
7. When you've finished asking, thank the spirits and then ask them to leave.
8. Cleanse yourself and your ritual space.
9. Now, analyze what you've written in the book. If you don't think you wrote anything serious, don't worry about it. With time, you'll

get clearer, better information using this method. Just make sure to practice often.

Some of the messages that come through may make sense in terms of sentence structure, but their meaning may not be clear right away or until later when something happens; then, you may suddenly know what it was about. After the session, you may ponder these automatic writings, but don't beat yourself up for not knowing. Trust that all will be revealed.

Communication through Scrying

Scrying involves looking at a reflective object to see things in it. You may see images, words, the past, the present, the future, and more. Scrying is a craft practiced with various mediums like lakes, bowls of water, fire, brass, copper, smoke, etc. Nowadays, many diviners who scry use scrying mirrors, also known as black mirrors. If you'd like to make yours, you can get the materials you need from a thrift store. Most of the mirrors are round, but you can go for something square if you like. You'll need a picture frame with a piece of glass. The glass will serve as your reflective surface.

1. Clean the glass with a window cleaner, freeing it from smudges and stains.
2. Put the glass on the newspaper. You only need a sheet.
3. Paint the glass black with some acrylic paint. It's best to go for the paint that will leave you with a metallic or glossy finish, but if you only have matte paint, that's fine too. You may need to do a few thin coats, waiting for each one to dry before applying the next coat. Make sure there's no spot uncovered, and you don't leave streaks. Five coats should do it, so you can no longer see through the paint if you hold the glass up against the light.
4. Put the glass back in the frame with the painted side as the back. The clear glass should be to the front.
5. Clean the glass once more to remove all streaks, and you've finished.

You can buy it online if you don't want to make yours.

How to Scry with Your Scrying Mirror

1. Cleanse your mirror by smudging it with some sage. This will eliminate any energies that are old, stale, and bad.

2. Bless your mirror and charge it by letting your hands hover over it and imagining a ball of white light moving from your hands to your mirror. Imagine feeling good energy flowing from your hands to the mirror if you can't visualize. You can also charge it in sunlight or under the moonlight during a full moon.
3. When you're ready to use your mirror, ensure there is not much light in the room. You can draw the shades and then light candles on either side of the mirror. Alternatively, you can just dim the lights.
4. Set your mirror up, so it's at an angle that keeps you from reflecting on it.
5. Ground yourself, and then take some minutes to get into a trance.
6. When your mind is clear and empty, gaze into the mirror. If you've got a question to ask, you may do so. Note that you want to look through the mirror or past it instead of right at it. At first, you may see nothing, but you'll notice colors with time. The images you get may not be clear initially, but with time and practice, you'll find they become clearer.
7. Practice for ten to fifteen minutes each time in the beginning, then you can try for longer later. Note that sometimes you may not get an image, but you'll get an intuitive nudge about what you're looking for.
8. Keep a pen and paper close to your mirror to note the important things you see as soon as you've finished scrying.

Chapter 6: Working with Ancestors and Departed Loved Ones

Now that you know all the necessary information about communicating with spirits, it's time to learn how to contact certain kinds of spirits. In this chapter, you'll learn how to connect with your ancestors and the loved ones you had who have passed on.

Many people come across ancestral spirits without realizing it.
https://www.pexels.com/photo/man-hands-people-woman-7189444/

Have you ever felt a chill in the air or sensed someone standing behind you? Have you ever looked over your shoulder and thought someone was there, only to find that nobody was there? You're not crazy. Our ancestors' spirits live with us every day.

Many people come across ancestral spirits without realizing it. It's probably best to have an open mind about these encounters because they can be powerful and positive. When you communicate with your spiritual ancestors, it feels like they are right next to you, asking you to let them be a helpful, positive part of your life. No matter how old or young you are — and whether you believe in supernatural forces or not — it's healthy to interact with the spirits of your family members who have passed from this world.

Ancestral spirits are more than imaginary friends and guardians. They're a living part of your history, part of your heritage. According to Native American traditions, they are a bridge between the dead and the living, and they talk to us so that we can share our stories with them.

Benefits of Connecting with Ancestors

Ancestral spirits can help you to heal from past hurts. Talking with your spirit guides or ancestral spirits is a great way to heal past wounds. These spirits are the guardians of your family lineage, which takes you back to the beginning of your tribe. Talking with them allows you to connect with everything that your ancestors went through and how much they suffered and struggled from living in a different era. Your ancestors' spirits are deeply connected to their stories and want us to talk about them so we can learn from their struggles and mistakes.

Ancestral spirits can free you from negative thoughts or emotions like fear, anger, or other painful feelings. It's not uncommon for people to feel emotions they don't want or need to. An ancestral spirit can help you to let go of negative thoughts and feelings that might be holding you back from other goals in your life.

An ancestral spirit can support you in reaching your goals, whether it's a career, spiritual growth, or anything else important to you. An ancestral spirit can help bring your dreams into reality. This happens when our ancestors are given a voice, and the spirits speak directly and powerfully into our lives, giving us strength and the inner resolve we need to make our dreams come true.

Ancestral spirits can tell you exactly what you need to hear. When we ask our ancestors' spirits to talk with us, they don't give us platitudes or say, "Everything's going to be okay." Rather, they are brutally honest and will not hold back any truth. Sometimes this can be painful, but often the words we need to hear most are the ones that hurt us the most.

Connecting with Your Ancestors

Before you get into the process of reaching out to your ancestors, the first thing you should consider doing is looking into your genealogical tree. If this isn't possible for you, don't sweat it. It's just an optional step that can be useful for establishing a connection with your ancestors. For instance, learning about who they are might help you know their favorite things, so you know what offerings to make to them that would please them. Here are some tips for finding out about your roots:

Organize What You Learn

Your first weeks will give you many results, and you'll need a way to organize what you learn. You should use an online genealogical database to help you before you start your research. You can find many for free or at a fee, including the popular Ancestry.com, an excellent choice because tens of millions of family trees are on their database. The branches may be useful to you as you search.

Look for Clues in Your Home

You should consider everything around you. Look out for patterns and check out your family history. Some clues about who you are could be hidden in plain sight. You can check out the basement, drawers, the attic, personal documents, letters, and anything else that's in storage that may help. Look at dated items and documents, and check your family albums and memorabilia. Look at diaries, report cards, and so on. You should get your relatives involved in the process and let them know your motivation.

Speak with the Elders

Older relatives will have more information than you do. The older, the better, as they'll act as a link to previous generations you may not have met. Even when you've got the facts about your entire family, you should ask your elders questions and record them because they may give you even more important details. Seek their help to identify faces and places in old pictures, as this could lead to stories that give you even more information to work with. Ask about your grandparents, great-grandparents, and other relatives. Ask for full names, siblings, where they were born, when they were born, their ethnicities and nationalities, what they did for a living, where they were buried, and so on. Be respectful as you ask these questions. If someone refuses to answer certain things, you should move on to something else rather than persist and offend them. You may be able to find the missing pieces through your own research.

Use the Internet

Now that you've got all the information from questioning your relatives and sleuthing at home, it's time to turn to the Internet. You can use different services, resources, and more to help you with your genealogy. FamilySearch is a good free resource, run by the Mormon Church, and is a nonprofit. They've been in the business of collecting records globally for the past 100 years, and they update their online records with tens of millions of entries each week. Look into their books, publications, microfilm catalog, etc.

Get a DNA Test

National Geographic offers Geno 2.0, a kit that can help you discover more about who you are without needing to follow a paper trail. You'll learn about how your ancient ancestors migrated eons ago and where your roots truly are. You want a DNA testing service with an impressive database of already tested people and the option to store your DNA samples for free in case you'd like another test later. You should beware of your decision to get tested, as you may learn a lot about your immediate family members or yourself that you're not prepared for.

Socialize

Social media will be good for you in this case. You can connect with people with the same surnames as you and also look for local organizations, archives, and genealogical services present in your ancestor's original hometown. You'll find it very useful to speak to strangers you share the last name with if they haven't had to deal with too many people asking those same questions.

Keep a Handle on Your Expectations

Most TV shows tend to sensationalize the process of discovering genealogy information. As a result, some people think they'll find out they were related to some great person who lived in the past. The odds are your origins are very ordinary, and there's nothing wrong with that. Those people still made a difference in the world because, after all, is said and done, you wouldn't be here without them.

Don't Quit

Finding out about your roots is very rewarding. When you put in the time and work and continue to push through despite obstacles, you'll be glad you did. This is because you'll be able to establish a richer connection with your ancestors. If you're wondering how long the process will take, remember that the more you look into your past, the more ancestors you'll learn about. In other words, the process of discovering your lineage never ends. So enjoy it. When you begin connecting with your ancestral spirits, you can ask them questions you've been unable to find the answers to. They'll be more than happy to fill in the blanks since you've taken such a deep interest in them and their lives.

How to Connect with Your Ancestor Spirits

Here's a ritual you can use to connect with your ancestor spirits.

1. **Begin by grounding yourself:** You must have the right energy to perform this ritual. Therefore, it is important to ground yourself. Are you feeling tired or not quite present? You should use the grounding ritual from the previous chapter to draw energy from the earth to fuel you. Feeling all over the place and overly excited? Or do you feel like you have picked up other people's energies over the day? Then let the earth absorb the energy from you as you ground yourself.

2. **Cleanse the space you'll be working with:** Burn sage and smudge the room, walking from one corner to the next. Alternatively, you could sprinkle or spritz salt water all over the space or create a circle with salt on the floor around the area you'll be working in. This is meant to keep out any negative or unwanted energies around you.

3. **Cleanse the tools you intend to work with:** All you have to do is use sage or saltwater. Make sure you have your pen and paper or other tools ready to take notes as soon as you're done channeling your ancestral spirits or connecting with them. After cleansing them, set them up for use.

4. **Cleanse yourself:** When you've cleansed the space, cleanse yourself by smudging with sage or using salt water. If you like, you can draw a protective symbol on your forehead with your forefinger after dipping it into salt water or the ashes left behind by the burnt sage.

5. **Get into a trance:** Begin by focusing on your breath in meditation, and then follow your instructions earlier in the book. Keep your

intention in the back of your mind as you slip into a trance.

6. **Feel for the energy of your ancestors:** Now you're in a trance. Seek out your ancestors by connecting with their energy. By sitting in silence, you can tell when they're around. There may be a charge in the air, a change in pressure, some sound, or other things.

7. **Set their offerings before them:** If you know what your ancestors enjoy, you can offer it to them. You'll know what to give them if you do your homework on who they were and what they were like when they were alive. The offerings should already be there with you, so just declare that you've brought them gifts to honor them and thank them for showing up.

8. **Ask your questions:** When you sense they're present, you may go ahead to work with them using your tools, whether that's the Ouija board, your pen and paper (for automatic writing), your sound recorder (for channeling), your black mirror for scrying, and so on. Ask them your questions and expect them to give you answers. Don't push, and don't be impatient. It will take them as long as it takes them.

9. **Express gratitude and make your requests:** Thank them for the answers that they've given you. Use the opportunity to ask them for anything else you'd like from them, whether that's health, provision, protection, guidance, abundance, or anything else. Then, thank them once more for being there for you.

10. **Let them know you're done:** Since these are your ancestors, you don't have to dismiss them. However, if you want to, you can simply tell them at the end of the session that they should leave now. They'll respect your boundaries and do just that. This is the close of the session. If you don't ask them to leave, don't be surprised at phenomena happening around you as they love to let you know that they're always with you.

You can use these same steps to connect with other loved ones you know who have passed on. In the beginning, these conversations with spirit may feel one-sided, but you must keep going. Continue reaching out to them each day, and with time, you'll begin to actually receive information from them, making your effort worth it.

Why Gratitude Matters

In real life, you probably don't care much for friends who only show up when they need something from you, only to disappear once more without as much as a *thank you*. If you have a healthy self-esteem, you realize those aren't friends – they are leeches.

This is why you must express gratitude to the spirits who come to your aid. It's also why offerings are so important. If you don't know what the spirits want because you didn't get that information from your research or there was too little information to go on, just let your gut guide you about what to offer. You may offer food, drink, water, cigarettes, money, fruit, flowers, or anything else your intuition leads you to. If your intentions are pure and you've made an offering, trust that the spirits see your heart and appreciate you for trying. They may even offer information about what would make a suitable offering for subsequent channeling sessions.

Helpful Tips to Keep Your Ancestors and Deceased Loved Ones Around

1. **Say hello to them** first thing in the morning. Say out loud, "Good morning, my ancestors. Thank you for keeping me safe during the night." Let them know how you'd like them to help you throughout the day.

2. **Establish a special place in your home** where you can go to talk with your ancestral spirits. It could be a small room, a kitchen corner, or even a special chair dedicated only to these conversations.

3. **Leave an empty seat at the dinner table** for deceased loved ones. Maybe it's someone who died before you were born or a relative who has recently passed away. Use your imagination to see them sitting across from you at the breakfast table. Speak with them and make them feel welcome.

4. **Pray.** Praying is a wonderful way to open yourself up and speak with your ancestors' spirits. It creates a spiritual field in which they can come closer to you and connect with you even more.

5. **Call on them during times of need.** Call on the ancestors for guidance and advice whenever you're feeling confused or unsure of what decisions are right for you. They will help you

find the answers you need and show you the path ahead that's best for your journey in life.

6. **Set up altars in your home**. Altars help you to remember your family lineage and show respect for beloved ancestors who have already passed on. An ancestral altar can be as simple or elaborate as you'd like it to be. It's an attractive place where you can leave offerings for them and keep pictures of those who have preceded you in this world.

7. **Visit their gravesites**. Make sure you take them flowers and fresh water whenever there is cause to celebrate their memory - a birthday, anniversary, a religious holiday, or the first day of summer or winter, for example. They'll appreciate that special touch of recognition from their descendants today just as much as they did when they were alive and well on the Earth plane.

8. **Make a homemade memorial plaque**. You can create one you hang on your wall or one in the front window of your home to honor your ancestors. Convey thoughts of gratitude and love for them every time you see it. Then, whenever someone passes through your home, they'll see it and think of the special relationship between you and the spirits who have already passed over.

9. **Create a space for them** in the house where all their important belongings will always be displayed, so their spirit is never far from where they were born and lived. Place their personal items on a shelf with a photo of them, create small altars, or all of the above. They'll love to see this spot every time they visit you. Take fresh flowers from your garden and fresh water whenever you can.

10. **Honor their memory at Thanksgiving**, Christmas, birthdays, and other holidays are times when many ancestral spirits like to come back and visit the ones who remain. This is a good time to ask that they give you signs that they are still around by moving something around in your home, hearing the rustling of leaves where there are no trees nearby, or seeing animals behaving strangely when you're thinking about them.

Chapter 7: Connect to Your Spirit Guides

Who are spirit guides? These divine beings are either assigned to people or chosen to help them grow spiritually, keep them safe, and guide them along their journey. Some believe that spirit guides aren't actual beings but are more psychological projections representing parts of the human subconscious, helping us feel whole. However, spirit guides are much more than that. They are real. You may think of them as being aspects of your Higher Self, if you like, coming to you at different times in your life to offer love, support, insight, protection, and much more.

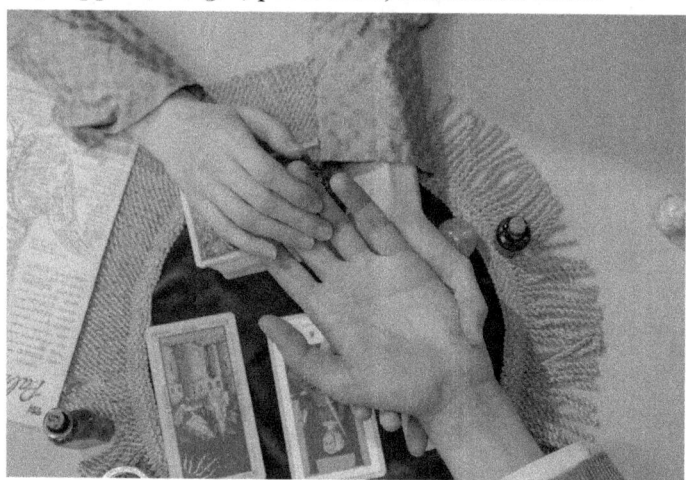

You may think of spirit guides as being aspects of your Higher Self.
https://www.pexels.com/photo/person-holding-white-and-green-floral-textile-7182586/

You may have just one guide or several. Your guide may be someone who once lived on Earth or hasn't at all. You may also have animal spirit guides. Regardless of what you make of the concept of spirit guides, the fact remains that everyone needs some support and direction in life. You would be hard-pressed to find a better being to provide this than your spirit guide. Your guide can offer you help that no one else possibly could, making it a worthwhile endeavor to connect to them. Spirit guides tend to make their presence known when you're about to experience a significant change in your life or when you need to be quickly rescued from something. You will also notice them when you're experiencing a rebirth and new things you may be afraid of.

Spirit guides are part of the forces of the universe that are meant to lend us their help. Your guide may be an entity from a different world, a god or goddess, a mythical creature, an animal, an angel, and so on. Living a life without being conscious of your guide is incredibly empty, and you'll begin to wonder why you didn't reach out sooner by the time you've read this chapter. Your spirit guide will show you what you need to know about yourself, others, and the world. They'll comfort you as no one else can, support you through thick and thin, lead you away from danger, warn you when something's off, teach you things you need to know to progress in life, and so on.

How Many Guides Do You Have?

You may wonder how many guides you have. Do you only get one? Often, it's the case that we all have more than one guide or at least more than one aspect of that energy. Some of the guides you have were assigned to you at birth. However, others come into your life later. It depends on what you're going through and what phase of your life you are facing. You may think of your guides as being split into two groups:

1. Major guides.
2. Minor guides.

The major guides you have will help you with your life path. They're there to help you with the main life lessons you're supposed to learn and your ultimate purpose for incarnating on Earth. On the other hand, the minor guides only stick around briefly to help with fleeting, daily issues that may give you trouble.

The Role of Your Guide in Your Spiritual Awakening

Your spirit guides have a major role in helping you awaken to higher and higher levels of spiritual awareness. Your spirit guide is meant to help you with your spiritual evolution. For instance, assume one of your guides is the Bodhisattva of compassion named Kuan Yin. The odds are he will show you how to be more compassionate and merciful to others and yourself. If you're drawn to the Norse goddess Frejya, she may be asking you to learn to make peace with your sexuality and to accept the facts of life and death. With Ganesha, the Indian deity with the elephant head, you'll learn how to be wise, clear in thoughts, generous, and prudent with abundance. Your guides can help you improve, especially regarding the emotional wounds, traumas, and cognitive dissonance you suffer in different life aspects. They can help you eliminate blocks in your energy that keep you small and feeling lifeless.

How to Connect with Your Spirit Guides

Dreamwork

1. The first thing to do with dreamwork is to work on your dream recall. To do this, every night before you go to bed, suggest you'll remember all your dreams in detail. Make sure you have a dream journal, a pen by your bed, or a dream journaling app on your phone.
2. When you wake up from a dream, don't move a muscle. Just sit and think about the last thing, scene, or feeling you remember from the dream. Then work your way backward until you remember everything. It is important not to move because if you do, you'll ruin the process of recalling your dreams.
3. Immediately after you've finished with dream recall, you have to write down your dream in your journal or record it. Start by writing or saying a few keywords that remind you of each aspect of your dreams, so you don't forget as you're writing. Then you can flesh out the details of each keyword after you've got them all down on paper.
4. When your dream recall improves significantly, it's time for a new suggestion. Suggest to yourself every night before bed that you'll

connect with your spirit guides. It may happen the first night or several later. However, it's going to happen. You can note things you want to ask them and write the answers in your journal as soon as you awaken.

5. Note their energy signatures. This way, you can seek them out in your waking life by feeling for that energy and holding it.

Affirmations

Affirmations are positive statements that you repeat to yourself frequently. Repeating them over and over again can help change the thoughts you think of yourself, which in turn will help you change your behavior. When you communicate with your guides, affirm that it is a positive and good experience. Use affirmations when you wake up in the morning or evening before going to sleep. You can also write them down for later use and read them whenever it is convenient. Affirmations are meant to help change your subconscious assumptions so that you achieve a state of greater self-esteem, happiness, health, and well-being. You can affirm that you always easily connect with your spirit guides and receive their messages clearly and often before using affirmations. Putting yourself in a light trance before starting is best.

Bibliomancy

Bibliomancy, or divination through books, has been around since ancient times. You'll be able to receive guidance as long as you have a choice of books on hand. You can choose a book about the skills and knowledge you want to acquire. It's also important that you keep it near you at all times. Bibliomancy is an effective way in which to communicate with your guides effectively and safely. Bibliomancy involves asking your guides for guidance and getting the answer to your questions through the words in the book. You can use it, especially when you're new to spirit work or having difficulty gathering enough information about something. You can read different books, think of specific questions you have, and ask them with faith that the answers that come back will help you in some way. Here's how to use this method:

1. Ground yourself.
2. Cleanse yourself, your space, and your book.
3. Sit and get into a trance state.
4. Focus on your intention to connect with your spirit guides.

5. When you feel their presence, bring your question to mind and ask it.
6. Hold the book out in front of you and sit with your eyes closed while you continue to focus on the question.
7. When you feel the spirits are ready for you, open the book to any random page. Read the first thing your eyes fall on, whether at the top, bottom, or middle of the page.

Candle Work

Candles are powerful. They involve the element of fire, and you can use the power of fire to connect you to the subtle energies of your spirit guides. Here is an explanation:

1. **Obtain candles**: If you don't have a burning need for candles, you can easily find them at your local supermarket or craft store. The easiest way to obtain candles is to buy various colors, sizes, and shapes. You can also opt to use tea lights.
2. **Create a safe space**: It's also crucial that while you're performing candle work, you create a safe space where no one can disturb you. You must turn off the phones so no one will disturb or distract your train of thought. You should also position yourself somewhere comfortable where you won't be distracted or bothered by outside forces.
3. **Ground yourself**: Grounding yourself before connecting with your spirit guides is also a good idea. Grounding is like a preparation for connecting with your guides. It's an age-old practice meant to ensure that you won't be pulled into the astral plane while being susceptible to energies that shouldn't be there. Grounding can help you prepare for your connection with your spirit guides and protect you from any unwanted or malicious entities. The simplest way to ground yourself is by taking deep breaths, visualizing white light surrounding your body, and encasing it in white light.
4. **Light the candles**: Once you've created a safe space, it's time to light them using a lighter or matches. The number of candles you light should be based on your intuition. Place the candles around in a circle. You must treat the candles with respect, especially because they have a symbolic meaning and represent your spiritual connection to certain forces in the universe.

5. **Ask for guidance:** Ask your guides to manifest before you by calling out their names as clearly and distinctly as possible. Take note of any sensations you feel to discern whether they're communicating with you. If they're already communicating with you, pay close attention to their messages, and record them in your journal later on so that you don't forget anything important.
6. **Thank your guides**: When you've finished connecting with them, thank them for what they've done and continue to do for you.
7. **Close the session:** Let your guides know that you've finished with them for the time being, and then put out the candle flames using a snuffer or let them burn down completely. Whatever you do, don't blow out the candle with your breath.

Keeping the Connection Alive

1. **Show respect:** Some people have problems with their spirit guides because they don't show them enough respect. You should never think you can talk to your guides in any way you choose. Remember that everyone has their own boundaries and limits, and this includes your guides.
2. **Ask your guides for help**: If you want to ensure that you can keep your spirit guides with you, then you should never be too shy to ask for their help or assistance whenever you need it. You can also ask for their help to maintain your friendship with them.
3. **Take time to connect with them:** Make sure you take the time to connect with them as often as you can, and you should also make sure that you always show them respect and care.
4. **Maintain a spiritual journal:** It's also a good idea to maintain a journal so you can record the messages from your guides and anything else that comes up in future sessions.
5. **Practice gratitude:** Practicing gratitude is another way to ensure that you can maintain a good connection and continue experiencing their guidance. Another important thing here is that you shouldn't be too embarrassed to express your gratitude, and this is because your guides are also grateful for the fact that you're meeting them at all.

Your spirit guides are not just characters that only come to your aid when you're in a state of distress. They're with you as allies throughout your life and should be treated with the utmost respect. You can do this by following some of the tips listed above, and by doing so, you'll be able to keep your connection with them alive.

Chapter 8: Contacting Angels

There are multitudes of angels, far too many to keep track of. The easiest of them all to reach out to is your guardian angel. But, before getting into who the guardian angel is, you need to learn who angels are in general.

There are multitudes of angels, far too many to keep track of.
https://www.pexels.com/photo/white-ceramic-figurine-of-angel-illustration-52718/

Who Is an Angel?

Angels are beings with extraordinary power who are in service of the Source that creates all worlds. They can help people in different ways. "Angel" is a word that comes from *angelos*, a Greek word that means "messenger." They act as messengers of the divine, healers, protectors, and more. When they appear on Earth, they either take on human form or show themselves in full glory. This implies that angels could be around you, showing up in disguise. They also tend to have a glow about them.

According to Islam, Christianity, and Judaism, angels are particular about serving the God responsible for creating them. In Islam, it's said that the angels are faithful in their service, but in Christianity, there are records of angels opting to rebel against their God. In Buddhism and Hinduism, and some of the forms of New Age spirituality, it's said that angels are beings who have worked their way up the totem pole of spirituality, making their way to the highest of realms by going through tests. They continue to evolve, gaining strength and wisdom even after they've achieved their status as angels.

Angels can also deliver messages from the spirit realm to those on Earth. Usually, their messages are meant to offer comfort and encouragement. At other times, they offer dire warnings to their charges to ensure they don't find themselves in dangerous situations. These divine beings also offer their protection, guarding the ones they watch over so that they don't get into any sort of danger that would prove fatal or impossible. For the longest time, many stories have been of people being rescued by angels. For instance, there have been stories of people spiraling away from an accident scene to be dropped off a short distance away and safe from harm. According to Catholicism and other religious traditions with similar views, everyone gets a guardian angel assigned to them to be there throughout their life.

Another fascinating thing that angels do is keep records of everyone's actions. According to Christian, Jewish, and some New Age beliefs, it's said that Metatron is the archangel responsible for this task, working along with the angels known as the powers. In Islam, you have the Kiraman Katibin who handles this job, and it's said that everyone has two of these, one to record the good you do, the other to record the bad. According to Sikhism, Gupta and Chitr are responsible for noting down every decision people make. Gupta writes down the decisions that no one but God knows, while Chitr writes down the actions and decisions that everyone else can see.

Who Is Your Guardian Angel?

You definitely have a guardian angel, whether you are conscious of them or not. Not believing they exist doesn't invalidate their existence. Those who don't believe in guardian angels just chalk up the times they've been saved from danger to pure luck, but the odds are their angel was there looking out for them. Some people think each person has just one guardian angel that helps them all through their life, while others believe that you get assistance from various guardian angels only as needed, which means the angel you get is the perfect one for your needs.

Your guardian angel is the best angel to reach out to when you need anything, whether it's help, advice, companionship, protection, or anything else. The reason is that they're literally assigned to help you, which means you are energetically and spiritually closer to them than any other angel. Does this mean you can't connect with other angels? Of course not. When you want to reach out to others, it's simply a matter of intention. However, even in that scenario, your guardian angel is the best one to ask for help in that regard because they will know exactly how to connect you with the other entities you may wish to commune with. Also, since they've been with you all your life, the odds are you'll be able to recognize them with ease when they're acting on your behalf. It will be much easier for you to detect their presence and, therefore, to hear their messages.

Benefits of Connecting with Your Guardian Angel

1. **Reaching out to them permits them to act on your behalf:** The thing about angels is that they may be present, but they often don't step in to do things for you because they will never violate your free will. The times they do interfere, it's often because your life is at stake, and they have to do something to save you from yourself, someone else, or a dire situation you're in. So, when you connect with them, you can give them permission to do more for you than they already do, which will improve your life.

2. **Establishing a connection makes it easier for them to give you messages that can help you in your situation:** When you connect with your guardian angel, it's as though you're opening a little window of communication between the two of you, allowing them to communicate with you in ways that are much more direct and easier

to understand. They'll be able to make their presence known straightforwardly. You'll never have to second-guess yourself about which messages are just recurring thoughts or dreams and which ones are from your angel.

3. **Having a direct line of communication makes their presence much stronger:** When you connect with your guardian angel, you're giving them permission to be close to your side at all times, helping you and protecting you from harm. This will strengthen their divine presence. You'll feel safer, more secure, and much happier knowing that you're being looked out for by someone who loves and cares for you deeply. At the same time, it also increases your awareness that an angel is always watching over us.

4. **Having a guardian angel makes you feel less alone in this world:** When you know someone on your side whose sole purpose is to help and protect you, it makes you feel far less alone in the universe. It gives you a tool that helps you get through each day with ease and joy. Even if there are times when things seem bleak and bleaker still, just the knowledge that there is an angel on your side, who loves and cares for you deeply and wants only the best for your life, it helps bolster your optimism and make the most difficult of situations seem manageable.

5. **Connecting with your guardian angel increases your personal power:** A greater sense of security comes about with a greater sense of purpose. When you have a guardian angel, you have someone to turn to who can help you achieve everything your soul desires. They can give you guidance and help you along your path. Most importantly, when looking at things from this perspective, it's as if they are practically carrying half of the burden for you. All of these make it easier for them to carry out their life purpose. Those who believe in guardian angels believe that this is exactly what guardian angels are designed to do. They make our lives easier and better by taking away some of our hardships, showing us we can handle more than we think on our own, and helping us to overcome our problems one step at a time. Knowing you're connected to your guardian angel makes you feel more secure and confident in yourself and your abilities. With their guidance, you'll be able to make better decisions, take more effective actions, and move forward with greater ease and determination. You'll also stop being fearful, automatically protecting you from negative energies, making

it even easier for your angel to ward off bad luck or negativity that may affect your life.

How to Contact Your Guardian Angel

1. **Have a quiet moment alone and ground yourself:** The first step is to find a quiet place where you can be alone with your thoughts. This can be in your bedroom, where you can lie down, close your eyes, and breathe for a few moments. It can also be outdoors in the woods or by the ocean, listening to nature's sounds. Or you may be seated on a park bench, in your car, in the lot at work or school. The point is that you need to place yourself in an environment that gives you some time and space to think without distractions running through your mind and then do the grounding exercise you learned before this chapter.

2. **Get into the trance state:** You can do this by breathing and chanting the Om mantra, or if you prefer, you can just sit in silence and allow your conscious mind to dissolve into nothingness as you focus on your breath. While you breathe, keep your intention to connect with your guardian angel front and center in your mind.

3. **Feel their energy:** Once you're in a trance, you'll be able to feel the energy of the angel around you. You may notice some static in the air, a feeling of pressure, an odd coolness or warmth, or even a light caress on your skin. There are other signs your angel may be present, and you'll learn about them in a moment.

4. **Converse with them:** You can tell them anything you want to. You may not get immediate answers, or if you're psychically talented, you may be able to hear back from your angel in real-time. Either way, they have made their presence known to you means that they're listening to everything you say and will act on your behalf.

5. **Thank them for listening and helping out:** When you're done conversing with your guardian angel, you need to thank them for listening and helping out. The language of gratitude will bring about your success in manifesting the things you want to manifest in your life. Thank them for their constant love and support. If you like, you can ask them to continue to make their presence known and felt in your life.

Remember that there will be times in your life when you won't have time to ground yourself or follow this process to the letter. As long as you make a habit of connecting with your angel, you don't have to worry about following every step. You can just ask them to help you right away, and they'll be off to set things right again.

How to Connect with Other Angels

Sometimes, you may want to connect with other angels known to help with specific things. To connect with them, you have to work with your guardian angel and then ask your guardian angel to put you in touch with the angel you'd like to reach out to. Your angel will come through and honor your request.

Angelic Signs

The following are signs that your angel has heard you or is around you:

You Feel Energized and Happy

If your guardian angel has made their presence known to you and you're connecting with them, you'll often be aware of their presence without even needing to say anything. You'll feel uplifted, inspired, and filled with love from the inside out. Along with feeling so loving toward others, you may find that they are constantly showing you unconditional love.

You See Auras

Many people report seeing angelic auras around them, often describing them as multicolored lights or brighter than normal white auras. The angel's color may differ from yours, but it is generally bright and radiant.

You Feel a Flush or Warmth or Coolness

Your angel may also make their presence known to you in other ways, such as an odd sensation of warmth on your skin or a sudden cool surge of energy through your body. This is the feeling of their energy passing through you.

You Find Feathers around You

These feathers will often be white or a similar color to the angel's aura, and they are the angel's way of leaving a sign for you that they're around. The feathers appear for a reason. Each one is a message from your guardian angel.

You Hear Music

You may also find yourself suddenly hearing beautiful music or singing around you, which can be your angel communicating with you in this way.

Their voice will sound unlike anything you've ever heard and can have great healing properties through its frequency.

You Smell an Odd Scent

The most familiar smells around angels are often roses, lavender, or vanilla - but there is no rule about this, and it could be completely different for you. The smell is radiated by your angel to help you recognize them, and it can also give you information about what they're up to at the time.

Chapter 9: Reaching Out to Archangels

Different religions have their own form of angelology as well as rankings of angels. The higher ranks of angels have more authority and power over the ones below them, and the different ranks also look different, with different numbers of faces and wings. The following are the angelic ranks according to the Pseudo-Dionysian work, *Areopagite in De Coelesti Hierarchia*:

Different religions have their own form of angelology as well as rankings of angels.
https://www.pexels.com/photo/a-bird-flying-near-millennium-monument-under-blue-sky-13717918/

- Seraphim
- Cherubim
- Thrones
- Dominions
- Virtues
- Powers
- Principalities
- Archangels
- Angels

According to Pseudo-Dionysius, the archangels rank higher than angels, but according to the popular consciousness paradigm, archangels are the highest in rank. While the word "archangel" has strong ties to all Abrahamic religions, you can find other beings that resemble them in other traditions and Gnosticism.

The archangels Gabriel and Michael are recognized in Islam, Judaism, and most forms of Christianity. Some Protestants believe that there is only one archangel, Michael. You'll find mention of Raphael in the Book of Tobit, where he is seen as a chief angel, a view also held by the Eastern Orthodox and Catholic churches. Michael, Gabriel, and Raphael are honored by Roman Catholics with special feast days. In Islam, the archangels are Azrael, Israfil, Mikael, and Jibrael. In the Book of Enoch and other Jewish literature, you'll find mention of Metatron, considered above all other angels. However, this angel isn't widely accepted by all.

In some aspects of certain religions, you'll find that there are seven archangels, but their names tend to change depending on whom you ask. The archangels who remain consistent are Michael, Gabriel, and Raphael. The other archangels may vary, but Uriel is acknowledged more often than not and is written about in two Esdras.

Archangels in Zoroastrianism

Many anthropologists, theologians, and philosophers hold that Zoroastrianism is the earliest religious tradition that indicates a belief in the idea of angels. Also known as Mazdaysna, Zoroastrianism holds that there are seven Holy Immortals (or Bounteous Immortals) called the Amesha Spenta. These entities are all rooted in the Ahura Mazda, which is the most powerful of divine beings. These beings are similar to archangels, with immortal bodies that can move through the physical world. They offer guidance, protection, and inspiration to both the spirit and human realms. They are:

- Spenta Mainyu or Spenamino, the Bountiful Spirit
- Asha Vahishta or Ardwahisht, the Highest Truth
- Vohu Mano or Vohuman, the Righteous Mind
- Khshathra Vairya or Shahrewar, the Desirable Dominion
- Spenta Armaiti or Spandarmad, the Holy Devotion
- Haurvatat or Hordad, Perfection or Health
- Ameretat or Amurdad, Immortality

Archangels in Judaism

The Hebrew Bible refers to the archangels as the Elohim. In Hebrew, the word for angel is malakh, meaning "messenger." They are God's very messengers meant to carry out specific tasks. It's not common to find references to these beings in Jewish literature unless you're looking at the later material, like the Book of Daniel. They're talked about briefly in Jacob's stories, and there's mention of Jacob himself having to wrestle with an angel. There's also the story of Lot, who had been given a warning by angels to leave Sodom and Gomorrah. No biblical character referred to angels by name until Daniel. Because of this, it is believed that Jews only became interested in angels while held captive by Babylon. The rabbi Simeon ben Lakish of Tiberias notes that the specific names used by the Jews for angels were gotten from Babylon.

While there weren't any references to archangels in the Hebrew biblical canon, when Rabbinic Judaism superseded Biblical Judaism, there were certain angelic beings who gained prominence and soon had their own personalities, as well as functions they were meant to handle. While these archangels are considered the highest in the hosts of heaven, there was no existing hierarchical system developed. According to Kabbalist and Merkavah mysticism, Metatron rules above them all. Also called Mattatron, he acts as a scribe. He's mentioned in the Talmud and generously written about in the mystical writings of the Merkavah. Michael is seen as Israel's advocate and defender, while Gabriel gets several mentions in the Book of Daniel, the Talmud, and particularly in the Merkavah texts. Here are the twelve archangels according to the Kabbalah, all of them connected to a specific sephira:

1. Metatron
2. Raziel
3. Cassiel
4. Zadkiel
5. Camael
6. Michael
7. Uriel
8. Haniel
9. Raphel
10. Jophiel
11. Gabriel
12. Sandalphon

According to the Book of Enoch, seven holy angels are charged with watching over everyone, and they are considered archangels. They are:

1. Michael
2. Raphael
3. Gabriel
4. Uriel
5. Sariel
6. Raguel
7. Remiel

According to the Apocalypse of Moses or The Life of Adam and Eve, the archangels are:

1. Michael
2. Gabriel
3. Uriel
4. Raphael
5. Joel

Archangels in Christianity

The New Testament of the Bible has more than a hundred references to angelic beings but only refers to archangels in particular twice: once in the First Book of Thessalonians, Chapter 4, verse 16, and again in the Book of Jude, Chapter 1, verse 9. When it comes to the Catholic church, there are three, Gabriel, Michael, and Raphael. Archangels Uriel and Jeremiel are mentioned in four Esdras but aren't considered by the Catholic Church.

Archangels You Can Call On

Michael — the Defender and Protector of All: Michael is the most powerful of the archangels, and he continues to fight against darkness and evil so that the world can have peace. His name means "He who is like God." He often has a pair of scales to measure a soul's weight in divine justice or a sword engulfed in blue flames. His sword and armor represent protection, strength, and courage. He commands the Legion of Light with his sapphire sword in his arm. That sword represents wisdom and discernment, which you can develop the higher you go on the spiritual ladder. His role is to fight evil, protect souls from darkness, help everyone when they die, and see the souls on to their next journey after death. When you call on this archangel, ensure that it's not for something you can easily sort out yourself. You should make sure you're not asking to hurt anyone. If you're invoking Michael for someone else, you should get the person's permission first. This is the archangel to call on in matters of truth, protection, strength, and courage.

Raphael — the Healer: Raphael means "He who heals like God." This is the patron saint of all involved in the art and science of healing the sick and travelers. Raphael is responsible for healing all illnesses of the mind, body, and spirit, and he's a very compassionate being. It doesn't matter what sickness you're dealing with. Turn to him, and he'll help out. He's meant to guide the healers on the earth and is sometimes called "The Medicine of God." He also helps to get rid of demons who have possessed or oppressed people and protects everyone on each trip they take. Reach out to this angel if you want guidance and healing, or have safe travels. Keep in mind that he's more about laughter and the lightness of spirit, no matter how serious things seem. You'll know he's with you when you feel lighter. He has a staff he carries around, with a caduceus. Sometimes he'll show up as a traveler, a pilgrim with a bowl of healing balm and a staff. He's connected to the heart chakra, so when he shows up in visions, you should expect to see emerald green, which is the color of health and nature.

Gabriel — the Messenger: Gabriel is all about getting important messages across to people, so she works closely with journalists, teachers, writers, parents, leaders, and anyone in a position to disseminate information. She has lovely flowing hair of gold and white robes and always carries a trumpet made of polished copper. This angel is also good for creativity, childbirth, child care, and pregnancy. She will also help you in matters of love. Gabriel's name means "The Might of God." Sometimes she's also depicted as a male archangel, holding a lantern in one hand with a lit taper and a green jasper mirror in the other to represent the wisdom of God.

Uriel — the Flame of God: Uriel is the archangel that rules over wisdom and knowledge. According to the Secret Book of John, this is the being in charge of the demons who helped Yaldabaoth, the demiurge, to create Adam, the first human. Usually, this archangel is shown in his cherubic form, also known as the angel of repentance. He was the one who was responsible for looking at the Egyptian doors during the final plague so that those with lamb's blood smeared on the posts would not lose their firstborn sons. This archangel is often shown with a papyrus scroll or a book meant to represent wisdom, and it turns out he's also the patron saint of the arts. Uriel can be seen with a flame in his left hand and a sword in his right. His name means "Light of God."

Sealtiel — the Intercessor of God: Also known as Selaphiel, this angel's name means "Intercessor of God." He is known to play the role of intercessor. For instance, according to the Conflict of Adam and Eve, an apocryphal text of Christianity, this angel was sent along with Suriyel to save Adam and Eve from the serpent's lies. He's also the one who carries the prayers of everyone to the Supreme Being to be answered. According to Eastern Orthodox Christian beliefs, this archangel can help keep children safe, oversee exorcisms, oversee heavenly music, help destroy addictions, and help you interpret your dreams. If you're struggling with feeling cold and unemotional, you can't pay attention, or you continue to get distracted, he's the one to reach out to. He is often seen with his face and eyes turned toward the ground, holding both hands to his bosom as he prays.

Jegudiel — the Glorifier of God: Jegudiel can be seen with a whip with three thongs in his left hand and a wreath of gold in his right hand. His name means "Glorifier of God." He is also called Yadiel, Jadiel, or Jehudiel. Sometimes he holds a crown and the whip to represent the reward you get from the Divine if you're righteous and the punishment you get if you're not. This is the patron saint of those who work, and the crown represents the fruits of one's labors, especially in spiritual terms. He's the one who defends and advises those who work in a position where they have to glorify God, and he's also the one who carries the merciful love of the Source of all life.

Barachiel – the Blessed of God: This archangel carries a white rose, which he holds against his chest. At other times, he shows up with white rose petals all over his cloak, representing the blessings of the Divine raining down on one and all. He could also show up with a staff or a bread basket, representing the blessing of children. The Third Book of Enoch calls him one of the angelic princes, and the Almadel of Solomon calls him one of the chief angels. Barachiel is in charge of all guardian angels, and it is said that everyone must pray to him to get all the good things they desire from their guardian angel. He is the patron saint of married life and family, and he's seen as the one who looks after the children of the Divine.

Jerahmeel – the Exaltation of God: This archangel is responsible for inspiring people to deepen their spiritual practices to connect with the Source of all life. He is responsible for making you think about what you can do to get closer to your Divine Origin. His name means "The Mercy of God." He's also called Remiel or Eremiel, among other names. He looks after those who have passed on as they go along their path in the afterlife. Jerahmeel is also responsible for visions from the Divine, and he's called the archangel of hope.

How to Summon Archangels

Ask your guardian angel to bring them to you: You can summon any archangel you like by asking your guardian angel for their help with that. Summoning archangels can be useful if you want to improve some aspect of your life, whether that's your relationships, physical health, mental health, spiritual journey, and so on.

Say a simple, heartfelt prayer: You can pray to request their presence and assistance in your life. In the past, many have summonsed archangels by using simple prayers said sincerely. Just make sure your intentions are pure and do your best to ensure that you're asking them to come around for something important, not trivial things that you can sort out on your own.

Use their sigils: Another way you can summon the archangels is to work with their sigils. You can get into a state of trance and stare at the sigils while you sit in a meditative state, connecting with their energy and getting their attention. Sigils are magical symbols meant to help connect you with the energy of a specific entity or spirit. You can find the sigils for many archangels on the Internet for free. Simply print them out or draw them on a piece of paper you can gaze at. Here's an angelic sigil ritual you can try out:

1. Draw the sigil on paper to help you connect with the archangel.
2. Put the paper on your altar or on a flat surface.
3. Place three white candles around the sigil and turn off the lights. The candles should be the only source of light in the room.
4. Sit at the table or altar and allow your gaze to fall lightly on the sigil.
5. Breathe deeply and calmly. Note the energy in the room so you can sense any shifts or changes. Also, notice your personal energy.
6. The sigil could become three-dimensional at some point, seeming to rise off the paper. If this happens, do your best to remain calm and unperturbed, so you can keep staring at the sigil.
7. You may visualize the sigil instead of drawing it if you want to. Hold the image in your mind's eye for as long as possible and meditate on it. See it getting brighter and brighter, overpowering the darkness behind your eyelids.
8. When you sense the energy shift, this means the archangel is present. You can make your requests now.
9. Thank them after asking them for whatever you desire, and allow your attention to slowly come back to the room you're in.

Use their name as a mantra: You can invoke the archangel you want by chanting their name as you meditate. You'll need about ten to fifteen minutes. Just repeat the name of the archangel out loud or in your mind. Chanting aloud is good because their names have vibrational frequencies that affect your state of mind and spirit in good ways.

Chapter 10: Cleansing and Defensive Methods

Knowing how to defend yourself spiritually is a good thing, especially if you make a habit of interacting with the spirit realm. This final chapter will tell you everything you need to know about how to cleanse your body and home, protect yourself, and eliminate any unwanted presence or entity from your space or home. Before getting into all that, there's one enemy you have to beware of that could put you in grave danger if you give in to it.

Knowing how to defend yourself spiritually is a good thing, especially if you make a habit of interacting with the spirit realm.
https://www.pexels.com/photo/a-bundle-of-sage-smoking-7947722/

Beware of Fear

The thing about fear is that it is *low-vibration energy* that's very attractive to negative entities. If you go into spirit work with fear in your heart, you'll be a homing beacon for entities that want to cause you trouble or mischief. In fact, calling it *mischief* is putting it lightly because these spirits have been known to make life unbearable for those they latch on to. When you're not afraid of them, you no longer hold any appeal as far as they're concerned, so they have no reason to hang around.

Here are other ways fear can ruin your spirit work:

1. When you fear something new or different, your natural curiosity about the subject disappears. Fear sucks you in and makes you feel like there isn't really anything to be curious about.
2. When you're afraid, you can sometimes stop trusting your instincts. Whatever you are doing, if you don't trust yourself, it's easy to make mistakes or second guess your actions.
3. You can sometimes lose focus on what you are doing when you are afraid and allow your thoughts to run away from you. Scary scenarios start playing in your head, making you jumpy or distracting you from the task.
4. Fear makes it hard for you to hear your guardian angel or other spirits when they need to warn you about something or comfort you. This means that you can find yourself in situations you could have avoided by choosing to remain calm.

What do you do to handle the fear you may feel from doing something new? How do you deal with your nerves when entering uncharted spiritual territory? Sure, you'll have some fearful thoughts, but you need to begin conditioning your mind to ask questions about the phenomena you see. In other words, get curious. It's hard to be curious and afraid at the same time. Think about how you can feel more at home communicating with spirits, what you could do to deepen your relationship with them, how you may make yourself feel safer so you don't feel afraid, and so on. Considering these things and actively working on them will go a long way toward mitigating your fears and worries.

Why Spiritual Cleansing Matters

Spiritual cleansing cannot be overlooked for many reasons. For one thing, it purifies you of any negative or stale energy. Even in your home, sometimes negative energy can intensify, or the energy can get stale from a lack of movement, light, or air in your space. These stagnant, sad energies can cause us much damage in life. You may notice yourself attracting the wrong crowd. You may find that you're suddenly struggling with bills, illness, and other phenomena that aren't normal for you. You may find yourself dealing with nights full of nightmares, unclear messages from your guides, messages from the wrong sorts of spirits, a lack of mental clarity, no peace of mind, and so much more. Besides just getting rid of these energies, spiritual cleansing is good for keeping your aura pure and clean, making it unattractive to harmful spirits. Also, certain deities and other spirits are particular about how you keep your space and body.

How to Cleanse Your Body

There are so many ways you can cleanse your body. You already know how to use salt water, an egg, sage, or a green candle to cleanse yourself. However, it helps to have other methods handy, so you don't feel like you can't cleanse yourself just because you don't have the required tools. Remember that you can cleanse yourself by working with the four classical elements (earth, air, water, and fire) at any time. Let's go over the various options you have:

Smoke Cleansing Rituals: Did you know sage isn't the only thing you can burn to cleanse yourself? You can use the smoke of any woods and herbs besides sage to purify your energy. For instance, you can burn Palo Santo, rabbit tobacco, rose, sweetgrass, lavender, rosemary, cedar, juniper, and so on. It's a good idea to check in with your intuition to see what would suit you best. Otherwise, you may just choose whatever you have available. The idea is to have the smoke touch you everywhere, removing all the negative energies in you.

Spiritual Cleansing Baths: You don't need to use salt when you're doing a spiritual cleansing bath. You can use other things like teas, herbs, crystals, flowers, etc. Some other things to try for your baths are:
- Charge your bath water with crystals. Clear quartz is a good option. You don't have to put the crystal in your bath water. Just let it sit by the tub, and set a clear intention in your mind that you

would like to charge the water with cleansing energy through the crystal so that it washes away everything that doesn't belong to you or in you.

- You can charge your bath water with your imagination. Put your hands in the water and shut your eyes. In your mind's eye, see the water as nothing but pure white light. Feel the energy of this water. Notice its purifying power getting stronger and stronger as you move your arms through the water. Say thank you to the water for how it's about to cleanse your body, mind, and spirit, and then have your bath with the water.
- Add mint to your water. Mint is not only cooling but energetically cleansing as well. Adding mint leaves or tea to your bath water is a good way to amplify the cleansing power of your bath. You'll feel refreshed when you've done this.

Fire Cleansing Rituals: Some people like to work with fire to cleanse themselves. Some traditions practice leaping over a fire to cleanse themselves before doing spirit work. Please exercise caution, and don't try this method because you'll probably get hurt or catch on fire if you do. Rather than be this extreme, you can take an unlit candle and roll it over your body. Begin from the top of your head and work your way down to your feet. Imagine the candle absorbing the negative energy from you. Then light the candle so it can expel the negative energy for good.

Crystal Cleansing Rituals: You can use crystal wands of clear quartz or selenite to cleanse yourself. You have to wave the wand around your body and allow it to pick up all the unwanted energy that has stuck to you. When you've finished, you'll need to take the crystal out and bury it in the sand overnight, use sage or some other herb to smudge it, and finally, charge it out in the sunlight or moonlight, so it's ready for the next use. You can also keep your space clean by putting black tourmaline crystals in each room.

Tea Cleansing Rituals: You can drink certain teas to help you cleanse yourself. As an added bonus, the tea will also cleanse you on the inside. Try having kombucha, detox teas, and so on.

Energetic Cleansing Rituals: With this form of ritual, you'll need to be familiar with energy work like reiki. Use the palms of your hands to scan your body for any part that feels energetically blocked. Notice anywhere that has stuck, bad energy. Imagine energy flowing from the palms of your hands to those places. See the energy as white light in your mind's eye. If you can't imagine what it looks like, just feel an intense warmth coming through your palms and cleaning out the parts of you with energetic gunk.

Cleansing Your Sacred Space

It's not enough to cleanse yourself when you're about to communicate with spirits. You have to also think about the space in which you'll be talking to spirits. Your sacred space matters, and you cannot afford to let it accumulate bad energy or vibes. In the same way, your aura can pick up some energetic dirt. The same thing can happen with your home. Every person who has ever set foot in your home has left behind some of their energy. If you were watching something like a true crime documentary or a horror movie, you've affected the energy in your home and made it more attractive to darker energies and entities. If you are feeling sad, down, or angry, that energy lingers unless and until you get rid of it. Even a phone conversation with someone could add energy to your space. The energy of whomever you're talking to can linger. If you've been following so far, it should be pretty obvious that you've got to do something about keeping your space spiritually and energetically clean. You can't just take it for granted that it's clean and continue doing your spiritual work because that's asking for trouble.

Before you do any spirit work in your home or other sacred space, cleanse it. You should do cleansings regularly, every couple of weeks, or every month. This way, you can keep your space safe from bad spirits, vibes, illnesses, strife, and all that other yucky stuff.

Cleansing Your Home with Smudging: You can smudge with any cleansing herb you want. Don't just smudge yourself. Smudge your home, too. You should work from the top to the bottom of the house when smudging. Move from the back to the front. The first thing you've got to do is open up all the doors and windows. This will not only let in more light and air (both elements that have a cleansing vibration), but you'll also make it easier for the negative entities to get out of Dodge. Smudging while keeping the doors and windows closed will accomplish nothing for you.

Another thing to consider when you smudge is you have to address every nook and cranny of your home. Think about those drawers and cupboards you hardly ever open. Open them up and smudge them as well. Think about the corner behind that one door no one ever goes to. Check beneath the beds, the top shelves and cupboards, and so on. You must ensure the negative energy has nowhere to go and fester or hide in your home.

Cleansing Your Home by Asperging: To use this cleansing method, you'll need rue or rosemary. All you need is just a sprig. Dip the herb into blessed water, salt water, or holy water, and then sprinkle the water droplets all over your home as you declare, "I banish all negative energies from this space. Leave now and stay gone."

Cleansing with Floor Washes and Sweeps: A floor wash is meant to help clean the floor of the negative energies it holds onto. You infuse the mop water with herbs that purify your space, or you may sprinkle the herbs on the floor and then use a broom or vacuum cleaner to clean it up. There are many different recipes for making floor washes, but for the most part, they all have about three ingredients added to water. Some recipes require Holy Water or Spiritual Water, and others need Florida Water. However, you can just work with rain water or water from the ocean or a lake, if it's easier for you to get. Whatever you do, you don't want to use tap water, so please stay away from that.

To make your floor wash, you need to put the water you're using into a pot (preferably a non-metal one), add the herbs you prefer, and let them simmer for the next ten minutes. Then take it off the stove and let it cool down before transferring it into a storage container. You're more than welcome if you want to add essential oils to your wash. Just make sure you put them into the storage container first. Don't put them into the boiling hot water. Let the mixture sit for seven days in the sunlight, and then you can use it.

Before using your floor wash, you have to clean the floor as you usually would. Then, you can use the floor wash, beginning from the back of the room and ending at the front door. If there are other floors, work from top to bottom. Pay attention to the house's doorways and give them a good scrub. You can sprinkle some salt at the main entrances to keep away bad energies. The floor wash shouldn't be mopped up when you're done applying it. It's more like a rinse for your regular floor cleaning. So let the floor wash liquid dry on its own, which will activate its power. If you want, adding some of the floor wash liquid to your regular cleaning liquids is okay, which means you'll always be spiritually cleaning your home by default.

What happens if you have wall-to-wall carpets? You can apply the floor wash to the floor by spritzing your carpet or add a bit of the floor wash to

your broom and then use that to clean the carpets. You may also consider cleaning your carpets with cleaning liquid, including your floor wash. The following are the ingredients you can add to your floor wash:
- Bay leaves — for healing, purification, and protection.
- Basil — for prosperity.
- Lavender — for tranquility and peace.
- Cedar — for protection and healing.
- Pine needles — for protection.
- Rosemary — for exorcisms, healing, and protection.
- Clove — for eliminating unhappy energy, for protection.
- Juniper — for healing and protection.

Here are some of the essential oils you can add to your floor wash:
- Pine — for prosperity, purification, protection, and healing.
- Dragon's blood — for exorcisms, protection, and purification.
- Patchouli — for prosperity.
- Camphor — for purification.
- Eucalyptus — for healing.
- Cinnamon — for prosperity.
- Lemon grass — for purification.
- Birch — for healing.

Light Cleansing Ritual: Some people enjoy sitting in the dark, even on a nice sunny day, for some reason. If this is you, you need to learn to love the light and begin opening your windows so you can let the light in. The thing about sunlight is that its cleansing ability is extremely powerful. It's so powerful that it sends negative spirits scuttling away for dear life. So make a point of having a home that is bright and full of natural light. Start opening the blinds, and you'll hardly have to worry about negative energy accumulating in your space.

Broom or Besom Cleansing: You can use a special broom (called a besom) to sweep out the bad energy in your space. There are also smaller forms of this broom that you can use to sweep your personal aura from the top of your head to your feet.

Bell Cleansing Ritual: Did you know that sound is an excellent way to cleanse your space and yourself? It's true. You can use certain high-vibration sounds to send negative spirits out of your home. You can play or work with these sounds using chanting, clapping, singing bowls, gongs, bells, and ancient music (think Celtic, Buddhist, and Native American music, Gregorian chants, and so on). These things will keep your space clean and free from unwanted spiritual guests.

Essential Oil Diffusion: You can diffuse essential oils like rosemary, lavender, lemon grass, etc. The smell is another great way to keep your home clean and safe for spirit work.

Making Up Your Own Cleansing Rituals

You can test out all the rituals you've been given to find out what resonates with you the most. For instance, you may prefer an herbal spiritual cleansing bath and then clear out your personal space with sweeping and smudging. It's important to figure out what works best for you so that when you're doing intense spirit work, you know you've covered all your bases, and you don't have to waste time or energy being afraid that the cleansing method you chose isn't quite suitable or enough.

When to Cleanse

You know why cleansing matters. What you may not know is when the right time is to cleanse. Use the following as a guide of sorts:

- Cleanse yourself and your space once a month. Do this preferably during the New Moon or the Waning Moon. You can use an app to find out which phase the moon is in before you do so.
- When you've just recovered from an illness or injury or had to deal with misfortune or death, you should cleanse yourself. Cleanse your home, too.
- When a new season is about to begin, do a cleansing ritual. This will encourage new, vibrant energy full of blessings to flow toward you.
- Before you do any major spirit work, you must cleanse yourself and your home.
- Cleanse yourself after you're done with the spirit work. The same applies to your home.
- Cleanse your home when visitors leave it. Even if the visitors were little babies, cleanse your space.

- Cleanse yourself at least once a week as a form of spiritual maintenance.
- You should do a cleanse whenever you get the sense that you're heavy or your space seems heavy.
- If you're dealing with many emotions, cleanse yourself and your home.
- Whenever a major argument, fight, or misunderstanding occurs, it is important to do a cleanse immediately.

Protection Rituals

Protection rituals are vital for keeping you safe from any negative energy you may be confronted with. Here are some simple and powerful rituals you can do to keep your energy and space protected.

Use Crystals: The best crystals for the job are tourmaline and obsidian, as they're great at absorbing negative energy from their environment. You can create a protection grid with obsidian or black tourmaline. This is the process:

1. Ground yourself first.
2. Take four crystals in both hands and lift them to your Ajna or third eye chakra, which is above your eyes in the middle of both brows on your forehead. In your mind, get clear on your intention for the ritual you're about to do. Then say, "I now program this crystal grid to keep me safe."
3. After this, put the crystals in your home's four corners or cardinal directions. You should have one at the front door, so bad energies can't get in.

Use herbs and salt: The best salt for this is pink Himalayan salt. You can take a bowl of the stuff around your home and sprinkle it everywhere. You can also try the following to incorporate herbs:

1. Get a piece of paper and write "Protection" on it.
2. Put that paper into a fireproof bowl.
3. Put a pinch of salt on the paper, and then drop dill, rosemary, and bay leaves into the bowl. The herbs should be dry.
4. Let your hands hover over the bowl and, in your mind, think about your intention to stay protected.

5. When you're ready, set the contents in the bowl on fire. Please keep a watchful eye on them as they burn.
6. Grind the remnants in the bowl with a mortar and pestle when it's all totally burned. Then put the mixture in your home. This potent ritual will keep your home safe for an entire year.

Full Moon Protection Ritual: You're going to harness the power of the full moon to keep away all negative entities and energies. Here's how it works.

1. Find somewhere you can sit in silence and where you won't be bothered or distracted. You may smudge the place first if you like. Or envision white light or a warm sensation that clears the space.
2. Close your eyes and meditate, keeping your attention on the moonlight.
3. When you're ready, write on paper the stuff you want to eliminate from your life.
4. Read what you've written aloud, and as you do so, see the negative charge behind these things being released to the universe (or know that it's done if you can't visualize).
5. Take a crystal (obsidian or black tourmaline) and hold it in your left hand. Remain in meditation, contemplating positive energy, until you feel safe and can end the meditation.

Banishing Spirits

Banishing spirits is all about exorcizing them from your space. Sometimes during your spiritual work, some spirits defy you and make themselves at home, slipping through the cracks in your defense. Sometimes, they're there not as a result of your work but because they've been sent to you by someone who doesn't mean you well. Wherever these beings are from, the fact is that you need to get rid of them as soon as possible. Here's what you need to do:

1. Cleanse yourself.
2. Go around your home from top to bottom, back to front, sprinkling salt water or burning sage from one corner to the next. As you do this, say aloud to the spirit, "You're not welcome here, and you were not invited. Leave with immediate effect and never return." You must speak with firmness and do away with fear. You hold power here because they're on your turf and shouldn't be.

3. Next, invoke your ancestors, guardian angel, or any other positive force you want to come into your space. Tell them to take charge and destroy any lingering negative energy in your space. Thank them for helping you out.

Remember, there's no reason to be afraid of interacting with spirits. Ensure you follow the proper procedures, exercise caution, and be ready for anything.

Conclusion

Why is communicating with spirits a wonderful thing? Every time you request something from your spirit guides or speak with deceased loved ones, you open yourself up to the possibility of obtaining amazing gifts, information, and insight. You may also connect with your intuition and gain additional perspective on your life. Speaking with spirit allows you to access higher realms of awareness that can forever change your life.

By communicating with spirits using the information in this book, you will notice a big difference in both the vividness and clarity of your dreams and the ability to project yourself into a higher realm of consciousness that transcends time and space. This is a very powerful meditation that can be used on its own or with any other psychic development or spirit communication practice. You'll also begin experiencing many "coincidences," which are really synchronicity. Your life will be more aligned, and things will begin to flow much easier for you. You'll experience this because humans aren't just physical but spiritual. This means the process of meditation and connecting with the spirit realm leads to your spiritual nourishment, so you live a more balanced life in this world and the one beyond.

If you have ever wanted to communicate with spirits but haven't found the comfort level yet, this book should help you reach that point. It's said that until you establish communication with your spirits and guide, you are only using 10% of your potential. Communicating with spirits will benefit you greatly in every aspect of your life by opening up and allowing yourself to grow spiritually. To be a great communicator, you must take the first step. This is where this book will come in handy. It will guide you in receiving the amazing gifts spirits have for you. Anyone can learn how to communicate with spirits once they know how it's done and what it involves.

Sadly, more people don't speak with their loved ones and spirits. They pretend that they don't believe in anything that doesn't involve an afterlife, body, or brain when communicating with the spirit world is very real. You can have conversations with them just like you can have a conversation with a friend who's still on this side of life with you. The ability to communicate with spirits is a gift that people don't use often enough, sadly. The only thing you need to do to be a successful communicator is to be willing and open. When you start, you'll be incredibly shocked that it took you this long to open yourself up to the spirit realm, and you won't want to live any other way.

Your life is not only about you. It's also about everyone else who has gone before. You can learn a lot from those who have passed on. Most of the time, this information is given to you for your own good. Communicating with a spirit can give you answers to questions that will forever change your perspective on life. It takes courage to step out of your comfort zone, but it's well worth it if you are open and willing to learn new things.

You should give this book another read, taking notes the second time. This way, you can ensure that you're ready for the journey ahead. Spirits have a lot to share with us, and entering the spirit realm is worthwhile. So many wonderful gifts may be given to you, so don't miss out. Be ready for the wonder of spirit communication with this book.

Here's another book by Mari Silva that you might like

Your Free Gift
(only available for a limited time)

Thanks for getting this book! If you want to learn more about various spirituality topics, then join Mari Silva's community and get a free guided meditation MP3 for awakening your third eye. This guided meditation mp3 is designed to open and strengthen ones third eye so you can experience a higher state of consciousness. Simply visit the link below the image to get started.

https://spiritualityspot.com/meditation

References

Aletheia. (2016, March 10). Scrying: How to practice the ancient art of second sight (with pictures). LonerWolf. https://lonerwolf.com/scrying/

Board of Directors. (2013, April 11). What is a medium? Eomega.org; Omega Institute. https://www.eomega.org/article/what-is-a-medium

Psychic mediums. (n.d.). Osu.edu. https://u.osu.edu/vanzandt/2018/03/08/psychic-mediums-2/

Smith, G. (2017). Mediumship: An introductory guide to developing spiritual awareness and intuition. Hay House UK.

Spiritualism and mediumship. (2019, August 29). Understanding Voices; Hearing the Voice. https://understandingvoices.com/exploring-voices/voices-and-spirituality/case-studies/spiritualism-and-mediumship/

Wahbeh, H., & Radin, D. (2018). People reporting experiences of mediumship have higher dissociation symptom scores than non-mediums but below thresholds for pathological dissociation. F1000Research, 6, 1416. https://doi.org/10.12688/f1000research.12019.3

Wigington, P. (2013, October 12). What Does Scrying Mean? Learn Religions. https://www.learnreligions.com/what-is-scrying-2561865

Anthony, M. (2015). Evidence of Eternity: Communicating with Spirits for Proof of the Afterlife. Llewellyn Worldwide.

Berkowitz, R. S., & Romaine, D. S. (2002). The Complete Idiot's Guide to Communicating with Spirits. Penguin.

bor Klaniczay, G. (Ed.). (2005). Communicating with the Spirits (Vol. 1). Central European University Press.

Buckland, R. (2005). The spirit book: The encyclopedia of clairvoyance, channeling, and spirit communication. Visible Ink Press.

Hunter, J. (2011). Talking with the spirits: Anthropology and interpreting spirit communication. Journal of the Society for Psychical Research.

Leclere, A. (2005). Seeing the Dead, Talking with Spirits: Shamanic Healing through Contact with the Spirit World. Simon and Schuster.

Leonard, T. J. (2005). Talking to the other side: a history of modern spiritualism and mediumship: a study of the religion, science, philosophy, and mediums that encompass this American-made religion. iUniverse.

McMullin, S. E. (2004). Anatomy of a Seance: A History of Spirit Communication in Central Canada. McGill-Queen's Press-MQUP.

Hunter, J. (2010). Talking with the Spirits: More than A Social Reality?. Paranormal Review.

Virtue, D. (1997). Angel Therapy: Healing messages for every area of your life. Hay House, Inc.

Virtue, D. (2010). Archangels and Ascended Masters. ReadHowYouWant. com.

Virtue, D. (2002). Earth Angels. Hay House, Inc.

Virtue, D. (1999). Healing with the Angels. Hay House, Inc.

www.ingramcontent.com/pod-product-compliance
Lightning Source LLC
Chambersburg PA
CBHW070752220426
43209CB00084B/1263